Memories from the Father

Alejandro Rael

Copyright Notice

Copyright © 2023 by Cesar Alejandro Duran.
Known hereafter as Alejandro Rael. All rights reserved.
To contact the author, please visit: www.lionmedicine.com

No part of this publication may be reproduced, distributed, or transmitted in any form or by any means, including photocopying, recording, or other electronic or mechanical methods, without the prior written permission of the publisher, except as permitted by U.S. copyright law. For permission requests, contact the publisher info@crystallighthouse.org
For privacy reasons, some names, locations, and dates may have been changed in this publication.

ISBN (Paperback): 978-1-7636666-2-7
ISBN (Hardcover): 978-1-7636666-0-3
ISBN (Audiobook): 978-1-7636666-1-0

Publisher: Crystal LIghthouse Publishing
Book Cover Illustration by Lina Geipel.
Editors :   Camille Ostrowsky
                 Jamie Faro

First edition 2024.
10 9 8 7 6 5 4 3 2

For more information about special discounts available on bulk orders please contact the publisher on
info@crystallighthouse.org

*Dedicated to Lucinda.
Thank you for reflecting the depths of unconditional love.*

4

*Dedicated to my mom and dad.
Thank you for putting up with me.*

I AM that I AM

I AM woman too

FOREWORD	11
PREFACE	13
INTEGRATION PRAYER	16
INDUCTION	17
WELCOMING TO EARTH	19
THE CYCLES OF ABUSE	29
ALONE & RESENTFUL	51
RELATIONSHIP WITH MEN	59
RELATIONSHIP WITH WOMEN	93
SUPEREGO DEVELOPMENT	113
COMPLETE BREAKDOWN	127
THE WORD	141
HEALING THE PATH	151
ALEJANDRO IS BORN	163
INTERVENTION	175
TRUSTING LOVE	221
TRUSTING THE BODY	253
RAEL IS BORN	281
END OF TIMES - THE APOCALYPSE	313
CO-CREATING THE NEW EARTH AS I AM	327
THE MANIFESTATION OF NUMBERS	365
ACKNOWLEDGEMENTS & RECOMMENDATIONS	371

FOREWORD

Memories of the father, a self guide book back to the centre of I AM. Alejandro shares his journey on earth. An open dialog with spirit. Through separation we rediscover unity. This book holds a very powerful reflection and insight to the process of remembering. A journey from birth to the ever present moment of now. We get to witness the trials and tribulations of a soul seeking unity with the sacred father and sacred mother.

Alejandro opens up the uncomfortable agreements we make coming into this earth, consciously or not. Many individuals have come to earth to heal particular aspects of the human condition. We are children of this earth, we are loved and we are not forgotten. This book is a deep journey into the flow of Alejandro's life. It is safe to assume that we have all encountered levels of difficulty throughout life. We have either become victims of our past or heroes of our present self. We discover throughout this journey how the relationships with the essence of time and matter are powerful teachers. It is through our remembering that we begin to heal. It is through authentic conversations that we have clarity and freedom.

Alejandro speaks, with spirit, to the significant moments of his life. In the darkest of moments unravelling the light he carries. The evolution away from a victimhood mentality and towards a life long healing journey. A very committed journey to love, truth and the liberation from the outdated programs we are born with. We discover how this world intervenes with the sacred child and the lessons that he takes on to heal. Reading this story is a recollection of Alejandro's personal access to the akashic records. An esoteric library we can all access. Through the higher dimensions of reality we can see how each story interweaves and supports unity.

This is a journey to remind you that you are not alone. We are walking each other back home. Alejandro shares the wisdom he has discovered to bring him back into the centre. Through powerful quotes, guided questions or simply breathing through positive affirmations. This is a book for transformation. This book is an ally to observe what comes up and alchemise it back to love.

This is a book that has found you not by accident. It has come to help lift the load of what you have forgotten that you are carrying. Have a notepad ready to empty your mind and clear out anything that may trigger discomfort. It is not only in the witnessing, it is in the releasing where we find the healing. This book is alive and it has a way to speak to you. Honour your own process to heal. Make the most of the healing journey. Share your discoveries with a friend and may we heal together.

So we begin…

PREFACE

I AM so pleased to greet you my dear beloved. Thank you, dear child, for reconnecting with me, *your* father. Thank you for going deep into the sacred mother, in you, and getting to know me through her. I love you as infinitely, as I AM.

I will continue to speak through what we have experienced in this life. The journey to be as I AM that I AM, exactly as you are. Please, my child, share freely from *your* words in the different chapters when it clearly arises to do so. We are meant to bring unity to our connection through this internal conversation. As within, so without.

You were born with eyes wide open, and soon enough you became aware of the higher and lower realms. All inside of a home with so much love and security. We have chosen you, my child, because you carry enormous focus, light and love to see the unseen and to speak from truth. You have chosen, in this body, to be free and to experience all that earth is, and you have indeed experienced most of it. You have fallen deep into desires and have gone to the highs and depths.

You have turned over the stones that make up the deep human condition. You have shined *your* light into these dark realms and you have learnt how to love all that I AM. You now have accepted our union, and continue to transcend the depth of the collective *suffering*. We are together in this, and in all journeys.

Now, you know, that in the enormous love that I AM, you chose to experience the full spectrum of being human. Including the experience of harsh rejection and self-loathing that come greatly from these modern human indoctrinating mechanics.

This happened so you, and many, can find me inside of these deep dark spaces of separation, and see with clarity the full spectrum of light inside all that is. This now allows you to hold a clear space for *yourself* and for who is looking into their darkest places for their light. Thank you dear one. Please forgive me that you ever felt alone and unwanted.

I thank you dearly for choosing this with me. I love you for *your* bravery to discover the truth of being. We have gone to the limits of many areas in life. This is why we are writing this book. To show the limits and how to expand our being. You chose, my child, a family of considerable core strength and social *rectitude* to be able to navigate through the maze and fulfil *your* soul's purpose. Now you are able, you are supported, and you are free to write this book from its source.

Please, be with me and I will guide you through the ordeals inside the deep and dark waters that I AM. If you wish, my child, this book is meant to be written and read with intuition. It is not meant to be linear for you but organic.

Listen to *yourself*, as you are being guided by *your* own voice, asking to revisit a particular layer of *your* own story of existence, or asking to stop and bring forth the space that you need.

"I am writing this book for the deepest healing in me and for the liberation of all that I AM. I stand here and speak to that. So be it."

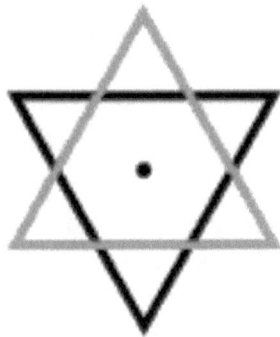

"May all Beings in All Worlds be Happy."

INTEGRATION PRAYER

I AM this body made from the Great Spirit that lives in me.

I breathe the Great Spirit in every moment that I AM present.

The Great Spirit is present in all living and nonliving things for me to see.

The Great Spirit that I AM is made of love and innocence that overflows its rivers of creativity.

I AM the innocent and loving child made from *Christ* or *Krishna* without any denominations.

I call in the highest perception of the Great Spirit to guide me through this journey.

I speak and write as I AM for the greatest good and the greatest good only.

INDUCTION

I speak to you, my child. Yes you!

As I am in this body, inside its 44th cycle around the sun that I am, as you.
I am creating this book for you.

I hear you, I feel you. Please hear me and feel me as I AM. I am going to tell you a story about you. A story as I remember it, and as I have discovered it to be. A story cultivated into this being, and transcribed from the heavens for you, my child.

This is a story about a man, a human as you, who came to earth to understand that I AM. Thank you, my child, for choosing this to be *your* life.

I speak to you from the Godhead, in you, that I AM.

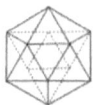

"May the healing and liberation of who I AM be also your own healing and liberation."

WELCOMING TO EARTH

It is such a courageous decision to come back to earth, dear child. From the peace and glory of the heavens to the *battle* on earth. It takes a lot of love to make this choice consciously, and not reactively as most people that do come back. You made this choice consciously, out of love, and you have arrived back to the density. The noise and the excitement of being alive on earth.

As you arrive, you can see this bright and disorientating light, straight onto your face. You can feel being handled forcefully by all these different people. All these different *humans* in your space, handling you without your consent. It can be quite a violating experience to be born inside a hospital, without the natural harmony, protection and nurture of the mother.

You can see all these happy faces, breathing and smiling. Right in front of you. You can feel all their thoughts, you can see their energies. They seem so excited to see you. Their faces are glowing from excitement. "What is this place?" You wonder.

We start this human life journey, inside of a robust and secure nest that you call home. An affluent and aspiring nest. A nest strong in mindset, focused and full of charming smiles. A nest that feels beautiful but somehow does not feel true. A blessed nest, with your two older brothers and your parents doing their best.

"I am a child of the 80s. I witnessed in that decade, the explosion of the *new capital system*. A way of life that on the surface looked very attractive, full of new toys and bright lights. Today, I am clear that in the depths, it was designed to separate us from each other, and ultimately to separate us from the authenticity of love that speaks from our soul."

Your first years on earth were short and sweet my child, as this chapter is. Most of *your* early years felt very safe. You felt loved and you also felt that something was off outside. Something felt not true. Everything was new so you could not put a finger on why people around you felt how they did. It simply felt off. It felt disconnected. Regardless, at this stage we can't distinguish anything more. The most important aspect for you is that you chose to come back to earth.

Thank you, my child. You were born into a particularly strong family unit. This home has allowed you to experience all that you have done, and without losing the centre in you. A family unit strong in *conservative views* towards politics, business and family.

This indeed was a decade of considerable mutation to the fibre of existence, dear child. You remember as a young boy witnessing, in *your* consciousness, how matter was transmuting its shapes and vibrations inside everything around you. It was as *things* would appear to expand and expand. Including you. This is when the plasticity of matter started to expand and transmute to the senses like never before. This is when the new *capital* perception took a strong foothold on earth, and the core values of humanity got challenged like never before.

In many countries the focus of adults was solely to accumulate what you call *money*. Now you are witnessing the demise of these ideas, and soon enough, the manifestation of something truly new. Something transcendental will become apparent to many.

The future is truly very exciting, my child! I need *your* energy, and I need *your* peace to fulfil my promise to you. Please listen to my call, I want as much as you, to be together with you, and our beloved, as one.

As many on Earth at conception, you were not completely desired by *your* biological parents. In *your* case because *your* mother, after two children, was desiring a professional career and she didn't know how to clear her energy fields moving forward. In many other cases, mothers on earth are abused, coerced, forced and shamed to have children. This is a deep emotional wounding in many on Earth.

You are not alone. As a matter of fact, you are blessed amongst the wounded. Please know that my eternally beloved, *your* sacred mother that lives in all life on earth, loves you unconditionally. Supports you unconditionally, and her deepest desire is for you to be whole and free from any wall separating you within and without. I invite you to continue to feel her under *your* feet, and I invite you to continue adventuring into nature, and continue listening to her and continue healing *your* soul.

I acknowledge that a fibre of feeling resentment to *your* mother, and not trusting the entire feminine thereafter, has been holding you down in *your* romantic relationships, and you have been disconnected from the source of love that you are, as I AM.

Disconnected, searching and yearning for the sacred feminine love outside of *yourself*. This has been the only thing that has made sense to the lack that you have been feeling. I understand this common condition, my child. I am sorry for these feelings of disconnection. This is how you remember to walk back home.

"In truth of the first person, I was born to countless blessings. In the core of a solid family unit. My mother was a great mother, her strict nature gave me the blessing of unwavering focus. Gracias mamá. You have given me as much love as you can. Specially, thank you so much for being open to my transcendental nature and evolution. I now understand that the unconditional fibre that wasn't met is because of the healing that we are doing together. You don't have to do anything dear mom. I've got this, you have guided me as far as you could.

My father is simply an amazing man. He is very

authentic to his values, charismatic and a leader of his generation. As his generation, rigid mostly in his views. A masculine lineage of apparently impeccable ethics and strong religious beliefs. I am so proud of him and how much he has accomplished. I am very happy that, in the present times, in his own way, we are sharing a path of transcendence back to the one."

My child you were indeed born full of blessings. Born into a life filled with privilege that you consciously choose for yourself. Thank you for sharing your blessings by writing this book.

"Inside the memory that I AM, I fully accept and forgive the knowledge of the world."

Share with us, if you wish, what you remember of this stage in *your* human experience. What memories do you have, my child, from this first stage in *your* life?

"I don't have many memories but I do remember how I felt, at that time. I remember being smothered with attention by so many people that I didn't know. I remember playing with my brothers but being too small to play with them safely. I remember being very happy and being very free with my expression. I remember testing boundaries, all the time. I remember being the centre of attention everywhere that I went to. I remember very joyful feelings."

You were indeed the centre of attention, my child. Inside the *spiritual definitions* of earth, you were born as an indigo, and into a family of what people on earth would call *leaders*. When you were born, it was quite rare for a newborn baby to come to the world with their eyes wide open, as you did. The nurses in the hospital were very excited. These were the first moments in *your* life, *your* deep and cheeky eyes started to show the love that you are in the world. *Modern* human knowledge, forced you to come a month prematurely, in a c-section, the umbilical cord and placenta immediately removed.

Thus as a spirit, in a human experience, *your* sacredness was not respected from birth and the boundaries of *your* sacred home penetrated. You were also not able to be stripped clean, with *your* mothers birth canal, from the external information happening during conception and pregnancy. You stubbornly chose to be born in mid August. This meant that you had a lot more fire that you knew what to do with, growing up.

Five planets inside of the Leo constellation was the choice for you. Together with a *Pluto Complex* in *your* Moon inside Cancer. This is why it is impossible for you not to feel and witness the deep *self perpetuated* chaos, still influencing the deep waters. The strong sun is how you have been able to do as much, and stay in the centre. This is what has made it possible to feel and transmute all the pain and fear from *your* feminine and masculine lineages with such boldness. It is *your* fire that allows you to have the magnetic attraction and power to liberate *yourself* and transform *your* being into our truth. Thank you for *your* courage and for having so much fire to give, my child. We share this quality, igniting love, and thanks to this love, it is that I AM.

Now we have transcended timelines and in a way we have freed our lineage from the past, and we have freed ourselves from this astral conditioning. Thank you for *your* commitment to serve me, as I AM and that I AM. Thank you for writing this book about I, as you, as me, and as all who are ready to listen to I as themselves.

This family was the way for you to go deep into the lower realms. You chose this family because you have been a seeker of knowledge, truth and power. We knew that this family was the perfect experience for this to be fulfilled. The ideal springboard for you to jump up to the true knowing and power of the eternal love that I AM. So it begins.

Such a strong family tree that you chose for *yourself*, my child. Thank you for choosing to have these blessings for us. A family of hard work ethics, strong characters to speak truth, and a solid backbone of faith and values. This core strength is what was needed for this to be true today. I recognise that our family was not connected and atoned with their emotions, and this evoked in you, my child, a lot of confusion and frustration. I know that it has taken you decades for you to understand that this was not personal to you and unique to *your* family.

The world created by the rules of men, has manifested a fundamental disconnection in most humans and their relationships. *Your* family was not the exception and emotional intelligence was not practised and developed. Vulnerability was not shared. Thank you my child, for all that you have studied and discovered to be able to get in touch with *your* inner motions. Thank you for *your* continuous practice that allows you to be crystal with what is, and thank you for being such a potent spark in the growth and expansion of many humans around you.

In *your* third year cycle on this earth, the flow of *your* creation, chosen for you to be fully awakened. Inside *your* own cycles you were seduced and sexually abused by *your* swimming teacher. You chose to experience this and learn early how a woman gets aroused with touch. You chose, as a soul, to awaken *your* kundalini, or sacred energy, early and become aware of the subtle worlds. This is what has given you early access to remember all that I AM.

Thank you for choosing this, dear child. This choice was very brave. Thank you for choosing to be as sexually activated as you have been. You, in presence, have activated many women and men towards their healing. Thank you for choosing *yourself* to slow down to heal *your* own somatic responsibility with *yourself*, and with everyone else. Who is also one with you.

As much as you did not want to come back down to earth, I am very grateful that you are here, my child. Thank you for the fulfilment of *your* soul. I am very grateful for *your* choices. For your persistence and for *your* faith in love. Thank you for *your* conscious choice to have another life in the human experience, and to have walked again through the mysteries of the heart. Thank you for choosing to discover and integrate all *your* past timelines into this one. Thank you for choosing love and connection through every crossroad of *your* life.

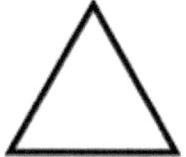

"This is a journey that resembles all journeys. A way through the ordeals of life. A path of perseverance and humility. The walk back home. Thank you, my child…"

THE CYCLES OF ABUSE

Readers please be aware that this chapter speaks into deep childhood traumas and this can be reactivating to your own human experience. Please check in with *yourself*. Please be gentle and patient with *your* processes.

This chapter speaks about the origin of the wounds entrusted to this body and how pervasive and fundamental they are for the human experience. Thank you, my child for leading the way for many. The wounds from childhood are sacred and they are key to understanding the greatness of being that is hiding underneath the human story.

What memories do you have from this early stage in *your* life, my child?

"I remember a sense of frustration. I remember being contained and emotionally suppressed.

I remember being ignored and not being able to connect to *my family*. I remember a feeling of not belonging.

I remember feeling unsafe with older or bigger boys. I remember feeling the need to hide, looking for refuge from being *handled*, *bullied* or *abused* by others.

I remember pretending that none of this was happening. Thinking that I was the only one pretending."

My child, there is no human on earth that doesn't share with you thousands of years of ancestral trauma. Even though on the surface, it may seem as uniquely different to you and that most are pretending, through personality, their actual experience. In the depth of reality, we are all healing together. Each one of us goes through different life experiences to wake up these ancestral wounds. Our woundings want to be seen, and they want to be witnessed so they can heal.

You see, my child, each one of us goes through different experiences that fulfil, in our own way and capacity, the deep desire to heal our disconnection from the source of life. These experiences bring forward the deep wounds of separation that we face as humanity. The fear of abandonment, the fear of loneliness, the fear of rejection, the fear of abuse, the fear of death and the many more fears that have been created by mankind.

Thank you my child for seeing the depth of who you are and for not being afraid to see this pure darkness as *your* own. Thank you for accepting and choosing the light and the word that creates from the void.

The first experience that brought separation to *your* perception is when you felt abandoned, early in *your* life. Two years old to be exact. This happened when *your* parents started to go on work-holidays, for a month each time to be exact. They left you behind with *your* aunt, uncle and cousins. Deep inside, my child, you felt abandoned by *your* clan, *your* family, and having been forced to be in a foreign space where you didn't want to be. You felt confused as *your* aunt wouldn't take you in her arms as *your* mother would. You felt confused because *your* cousins wouldn't protect you as *your* brothers would. You felt abused, as you were being bullied by *your* cousins and couldn't understand why they were being mean, as they were family.

You chose this my child, and you are continuously choosing You. Please remember this, every day when there is doubt and old programs arising. It is only unravelling from the deep desire to meet *yourself*. In the timeless perception of creation, you are facing *inherited wounds* as a man, and you are transcending the limitations through the feminine as *your* teacher. The divine feminine that lives in you is awaiting to be met and held in sweet embrace. You are building and embodying the divine masculine as I AM. It is guiding the way forward for many. The crystal clear container of the divine masculine that has not been present in the lives of most on earth.

As you are aware now my child: being born in the free-will on earth is the biggest blessing a soul can choose. It is also a traumatic experience from its conception. I invite you, my child, to bring forward all the wounds that we have transcended together. This will serve you to fulfil *your* healing promise to me. It will also serve you, the reader, to see *yourself* inside of this ancestral human story. A love to the unknown, as unsettling as this can be, it is where greatness and glory can be found. This is a story of processing the human experience, alchemising and transcending it to speak from the I AM, where you and I are one.

A couple of years later, you were repeatedly sexually abused by a swimming teacher. A woman who showed you for months how to masturbate her. Even though *your* parents were protecting you at all times, these events happened when they were not looking. As it happened and it continues to happen to children all over the world. This experience felt to you as a naughty secret. You felt aroused. You felt special and you liked touching her. You liked the perversion of experiencing intimate secrets that could not be told. This experience confused you moving forward, especially when *your* swimming teacher had an expansion of her consciousness, and she chose to stop playing with you. This was *your* first sense of sexual rejection. Soon after this experience, you developed an addiction to sexual arousal, a corruption in *your* essential existential system that you have been dealing with all *your* life. Thank you, my child. You are transcending.

"The more light one calls into being, the more darkness one needs to see and integrate back into light."

"Being sexually abused and rejected; as I remember, I was three or four years old and I was learning how to touch and masturbate my swimming teacher. She orgasmed at least once, and then she stopped playing with me, in what feels like a couple of months later. I forgive you swimming teacher, I don't remember your name but I remember how I felt. It was arousing to play with you. It was activating for all my senses to feel your orgasm. I got very confused sexually after that experience. I am sorry to all the women from my past. I blindsighted many of you. I got very confused and I thought I knew what love, sex and desire were."

We can share the trauma you have gone through, and we can portray you as a victim or as a perpetrator but this wouldn't be the truth, would it, my child?

Let us work together in this chapter to bring forward the highest of truths. The truth of you as creator of worlds. It is uncomfortable to be responsible for all that is in your life, then again this is how we become free. It is hard to witness the aberrations from modern times. The deep rejection towards being uncomfortable, and how it is creating a disconnection between us. The more that we can train ourselves to be comfortable in the uncomfortable, the more that we can heal the separation between us.

Stay here my child, I understand that you want to be in the now, writing about what you are dealing with at later stages of *your* life. It seems to be more practical and relevant. Trust that if we continue to write together, in *your* order of development, it will create for us the integration that we both yearn for. Stay here my child, stay with *your* first wounding, let's go in order of *your* life story. The holy child made of all that is true, is in you, and inside everyone. We want to show, through you, the truth of who I AM, and the truth of how we became *separate*; inside the illusion of the mind.

"In first persons' highest truth, I have been addicted to sexual pleasure since I was four years old because I chose to be addicted to sexual pleasure since I was four years old."

It has been an outstanding journey, very few wounded men in this world have connected and surrendered, as deeply and devotedly as you have. Thank you for offering so much healing to *yourself* and others. Thank you, my child, for recognising that you are a woman too. Thank you for going within to witness all *your* senses and what is below them. Thank you for recognising the sacred union within. This is the way to find lasting peace and divine presence on earth. Thank you for continuing to heal the separation with me and with *your* relations. It has been a challenging wound for you to overcome.

Firstly it was hard for you to recognise that it was a trauma. The old world thinking even made you believe that you *got lucky* early! Far from the truth, my child. You were violated as a child. *Your* somatic system was severed in the area of the right hip, not allowing you for forty four years to embody *your* full masculine presence, and not allowing you to be at peace with *yourself*.

Decades of internal discovery for you to be where you are now: - A clear and connected vessel where the Godhead that I AM, can speak and be heard. Now you are able to choose *your* masculine presence freely. This is a true blessing, not many have this choice. You are free to choose the identity of your masculine now. Now that *your* mind is wise, clear and mature. Thank you for going through the uncomfortability and being where you are. Thank you for choosing me as *your* closest beloved. May the divine presence be visible in you, walking on earth.

"In first person truth, operating inside a child that has been wounded, judgement has given me a temporary sense of protection. It has given me a sense of power with my environment. I am honestly so tired of feeling judgement inside of me. It is hurting me."

The web of judgement is here my child, exchanging the freedom of the soul for a simulated sense of safety created by the mind. Please don't worry, it is all part of my vision. Judgement, sooner or later, tires the soul, which has personality. It is then that the soul surrenders, and attones itself to the natural rhythm of the Spirit that I AM.

"I am waking up from many centuries of sleep. Inside of an ocean of judgement. I am waking up to a body restricted by a web of pain. Presently awake, I can choose a new light body breathing inside of spirit. I AM and, in free-will, I speak: I AM the divine love of transformation, I AM the violet flame."

It is perfect, my child, to feel this way right now, this is not personal to you. You are choosing powerful allies to support you through this liberation. A deeply wounded child, and its hurtful inherited judgement, has been pervasive inside of humans' decisions for ages. It is the wounded child that keeps the internal and external wars of separation alive. *Fighting to feel safe*. Thinking that we know better than what is right in front of us. This is what does not allow you, dear child, to witness the creator, the father and the holy spirit that I AM in You.

Can you see, dear one? It is simply a sense of protection for our wounded child, within, that sparks the battles of separation. In this *unsafe* condition, we have only been able to use separation to give us a false sense of control and safety over our environments.

The mind has been using labels and divisions to control the matter. Instead of using a peaceful heart to see beyond these fearful limitations, and be able to perceive and experience the unity of all things. This disconnection is what has been perpetrating the pain and the suffering. What you perceive now, that feeling of unsafety, comes directly from separating *yourselves* from the eternal being that I AM. Now you see, now you are coming back home.

"I write down to let go of my own perception of suffering and clear the Godhead that I AM."

I fulfil my promise to communicate directly to you, my child, and share the wounds of abuse. As it is, without the charge from the ancient story of victimhood, aggressor and significance that humans mostly speak from. How are you feeling right now, my child?

"I am now in a place of fulfilment, joy and devotion. It is a great sense of gratitude to be able to share myself and the details of the different experiences that shaped the depth that I have been discovering. I accept the human story in me, and surrender to all that is happening around and through *me*. This has been a deep and intense journey, coming from an old program of conditional love, based on righteousness and judgement. I am now in a new agreement of loving freely and learning to love unconditionally. Opening and strengthening the centre of love in the heart that I am."

Thank you, my child. Are you able to share details of the different childhood wounds that you inherited? Many will benefit from this. There is an old saying in *your* world '*Childhood is Destiny.*' However, destiny is entirely in *your* hands, when in communion with the child within.

We are going to start with the collective wound that marks generations. As a child of the 80s, our biological parents were leaders in the *baby boomer* generation. The baby boomers are the first generation to have access to the sense of freedom, and the last generation representing the old patriarchal world. The world of hierarchies. The world of, *should be* instead of allowing the *being* to simply be. The world where *what you do* and *what you have,* is somewhat the same as *who you are*. Such a committed generation, the baby boomers.

Three generations later and they are still desiring to be relevant in leading the way for humanity. Although this is not their story but *yours*, their story is relevant to you, and to all the offsprings from them.

"I want to thank all the baby boomers. You opened up the gates to freedom for *our* descendants. Freedom was new for you. It took you by surprise and you thought that freedom was the ability to accumulate things. I encourage you to trust in *your* true inner selves, and allow for the new generations to come forward and without any interference. We can continue evolving together to higher perceptions of consciousness, Time is of essence. Mankind has some catching up to do."

My child, please share *your* experience as a direct offspring of the baby boomers. *Your* generation is one of the last direct offsprings to them. *Your* insight might bring clarity to others of the impacts that we have not yet acknowledged collectively.

"Being born from the baby boomer generation felt quite overwhelming and disconnected at the same time. It is important for me to flush these feelings out of the system, by acknowledging the experience.

The baby boomers were the last generation that had their emotions systematically minimised and shut down. Mainly hidden behind rigid social and religious agreements. Their immediate descendants still received this education and this example.

This old world was alive in our senses with the relationships with our grandparents. The baby boomers where the first generation were economic ambitions had no limits for the many. The greed and the insatiability to accumulate wealth was very noticeable to nature. Their education expressed this grandiose perception towards natural resources.

It was very common to receive comments that would support our grandiose ambitions. 'The world is *your* oyster.' Was a very common saying in those times. The baby boomers were particularly strong in giving out opinions to others without their consent. Somehow it is the last generation where the many spoke, without respecting boundaries, and as if they knew better than the other person's own experience.

This was particularly frustrating as an offspring. They were the last generation governed mostly entirely by thoughts and reason, rather than by the experience of the senses. This created a sense of arrogance towards nature and sacred values that was passed on to us.

The family unit eroded considerably after this generation. The baby boomers were particularly afraid of dying poor and without legacy, being themselves born after the great war. To work hard and to live a family legacy became the most important value for them. Distorting the work-family balance that our souls' crave.

After decades of being a determined disruption to this generation, my parents and I have transcended the grip from these shadows. I pray for the same blessing to spread for the many. I hope that this discerning helps many to find peace and communion with *your* parents."

Moving on, my child, from the generational trauma from our ancestors. To individual *wound cycles* that you have experienced, in this life. We have shared some insight earlier but at this point, what is it that you want to share about *your* childhood wounds, my child? It is healthy to find a happy centre, and express from above and from below.

"Being bullied by the people I trust. Between two years old and four years old, my parents travelled overseas and I stayed behind with my aunt, uncle and cousins for weeks, that truly felt like months. One cousin is three years older. He chronically wanted to take advantage of his size and experience. I didn't have the security of the love from my eldest brother, always protecting me. This was the first genuine feeling of danger that I experienced. From these moments, was when I learnt to hide and to run away. This took on an early life pattern of feeling powerless with older or bigger boys, hiding from this threat and even running away. A cycle that repeated itself for many years to come."

"Winning it all to lose it all. My first *failure* in this life came when I was four years old. I demanded from my parents that I go with my brothers to summer camp that year. Instead of staying with my cousins. I am a force of nature so my will was done.

At summer camp, I was the youngest camper in history. I was so loved, winning many prizes. I felt like a king. This was until I broke a golden rule in camp 'don't swim under the peer.' I did swim under the peer, and I was punished by having all the awards I had won removed, just like that I was disqualified from receiving any awards.

That was strong punishment for a four year old to comprehend, and not have a strong reaction. 'This is unfair and I will show you better' became the unconscious blanket program that I created at that moment. Tainting from that point forward, any relationships with authority figures."

"What I love disappears. It took four decades to be able to identify this and speak. To defuse the program it had over me.

Our neighbours were three very beautiful sisters. In similar age gaps as us! *My* brothers were in love, The youngest was also *my* first love and *my* first kiss at five years old.

A love that wasn't shared with anyone. We would have our hiding spots where we would hold hands and kiss. We were so cute, and we both felt that we needed to wait some years before sharing our love without being laughed at. I was now six years old, and we heard the news that she and her whole family had died in a plane crash. It was surreal for me to witness this.

My brothers were crying for their own love connections with her older sisters. I was pretending to not feel the same. It was not until I acknowledged this impact that I was able to grief her. Four decades later. Today as I write this part of the book. I am truly seeing how this ungrieved experience was creating a block, deep inside, my flow of love."

"Being silenced and ignored. I was the youngest in my family unit. Five years younger than the brother before me. It felt that I was not a part of this family.

I have learnt since, that it is very common for the youngest of the family, when there is a considerable gap, to feel as an only child and to feel that he or she doesn't belong in this family. This was also a layer that significantly played up in my development. I grew up with the feeling that I didn't have a voice, or that I wasn't going to be listened to. That was also magnified greatly by the agreement I had with the *swimming teacher.* 'This is our secret, don't tell anyone.'"

And…

"Here I am, deep in the 80s, one full cycle on earth. Seven years old. How am I doing? Hmmm, let's see. I can now finally say in words how it felt then: I was sexually aroused like a dog around heat. Quantum leaps ahead, in perception, to the peers around me. Deeply afraid of being bullied by bigger boys. Deeply afraid of being in love again. Highly reactive to the law and order of men, and with a closed throat not being able to speak up."

So then, 'how are you?' my dad asks.
    "I am a great dad!"
I wonder, *how will this possibly go for me?*

"It will go great!"
I ponder and ponder...

Indeed my child, *your* life has been great, and it will continue to be great. I have been with you. It has been a roller coaster of experiences and emotions, or drama, that has been playing out for the unravelling of *your* soul. My dear child, as you, I am also coming out from this cyclical story, or cycle of abuse as you prefer to share it in this book. We are in this together. Beneath it all, below all the emotions, underneath all form, below time, thoughts and perceptions. There, we meet as one!

In the essence of vital energy is exactly where the *cosmic battle* for humanity is happening. What happened in *your* sexual essence is part of this cosmic remembering. The confusion of *dark one* seeks to invert the polarities, and, through the wounded feminine, attempts to take away the vital light in you. When the innocent space that I AM was violated, it felt to you like a ray of lightning coming up *your* right groin. Taking over the masculine sacral space in this body.

This intense force severed *your* connection with *Saturn* and the discipline that comes with this relationship. In turn, the wounded masculine jumped to the sacral space of the feminine, with a growing desire and spite towards the feminine that started to hurt *yourself* from the inside.

Now you see that this inverted *your* gender polarity. This is why when you were a child, you couldn't feel either as a man or as a woman. Inside play, when you pretended to be a woman it felt as natural as pretending to be a man. You couldn't recognise the flow in *your* body.

You are not alone, my child. Many children have this *confusion* that is not talked about but rather judged as *good or bad*, and reacted towards. Only creating more labels and emotions of separation.

It is a huge blessing in disguise to not be trapped inside the identity of gender. It is much easier now for you to free *yourself* from the deep and potent trap of gender identification or gender invalidation, that is another side of the same intentional gender *spiritual trap*. You are whole and you know it in *your* core. This *confusion,* as with every other mental mess, you have to go through it. We cannot bypass the steps of evolution. Honour the perspectives of sacred polarity, honour *your* biological polarity and honour *your* polar opposite within.

"May the polarity within meet, be in love and in honour of each other. May you find sacred union, my child."

You can now see clearly that all that has happened for seven generations, is stored inside of this body. Now you can feel it as well. As overwhelming as this can be. You have learned to feel and breathe through it all. Now, from this higher presence, it is *yours* to integrate and release, inside of *your* own practice.

You have the rare blessing of having a tender open space and being able to give new form, or not, to the deep masculine within.
You can now choose freely and maturely.
What does that look like?
Who are you embodying?

"I do not know, tho' I AM."

All other abuses that you have courageously shared with us, dear child. Has happened on top of this one sexual abuse. The beginning of the anxiety. The beginning of the insatiability. The beginning of the corruption started with this swimming teacher more than forty years ago.

At this moment in *your* life, you are feeling and witnessing it all. It feels overwhelming with all this activity within you. You've got this, my child. I cannot give you, or any of my children, anything that you cannot handle. Stories can be very activating to the senses. These stories that you have shared and the stories that you are in today, are activating. Please keep in mind, to continue to share all that arises for you, my child, yes you.

Share, with trusted humans, what arises for you, and remember to experience it through as much compassion as possible. We are all doing our best. It is not an easy task to free ourselves from this mental maze of suffering. Compassion is how we can, safely and gently, go deep into the ocean of love with our piercing bright light of truth. It is with compassion that we allow for life to unravel, without the harshness of judgement and the confusion of misinterpretation. You've got this.

Now, my child, today as you write these words, you are being tested like never before. All that you were holding unto has moved on, and all of your past fears are arising up all at once. Trust my child. I want to see, if you are, as I AM, ready to free yourself from these limiting beliefs. As you are free, I become free as well.

What are you facing, beloved child?

"An uncomfortable mask telling me what to say and how to behave. I am facing the illusion that I have created for myself."

What do you want to do, dear one?

"I want my actions to manifest your glory and *my* glory as creators, exactly as I am. What do you wish me to do?"

Doing nothing is what I wish for you, my child. I wish that you trust me with all *your* heart. Trust that I provide for you. Trust that I will guide you to glory. Trust that *your* glory is my glory, child. In the highest of truths, we are one. All that you need to do for me, to come into *your* life, is to create space within you for I. Space in *your* heart. Space in *your* home, space in your body and space in *your* mind. Space so that our spirits can blossom together, and space so I can drive the holy vessel that you are.

When you are ready, beloved child. You can let go of who you think is driving in *your* life. I will be there to take the helm. Follow the true desire of your heart. Learn to observe all that is in this space. Learn to soften and open the heart from behind. This is where the true door into our heart resides.

Look at all the air in the heart.
This superficial layer can be destabilising. High winds created from the unbalanced flesh that is lacking. The desire to be greater than existence and conquer. Look deeper, child.

What is the water in the heart saying?
These waters are *your* love story. Validate this layer. Travel across these emotions. Follow that purification my child.

What does the fire in the heart say?
The flame of spirit within. The flame that wants to create an open space for you to love one. Follow this creation dear child, this creation is you. This is the space where the true desires of the soul speak.

It is time, dear child. Are you ready to let go of all of these stories?

"I am ready, can you please guide me to be whole? Back to being true and in love of the highest good. Deep down, I feel undeserving."

Remember, my child. To remember me, please breathe with me. If it is hard for you to find me in *your* breath. You can see the qualities that I AM, where it all begins.

In the tip of *your* nose. In the entrance of the breath is where I AM. The clearest doorway into the body. We will continue this journey together. In any moment, the *separation* will be dissolved.

You have always been blessed, and you have always been whole. It is for us to remember that we are. Continue breathing with me, my child. We can enjoy the journey together. Let go of *your* expectations of how it should look like, and of what *your* sought destination is. This is limiting to all that you are. Every moment holds all the moments of creation within it. Every moment is the glory and the greatness that I AM.

This is a moment, as any other moment is. Continue breathing with me, my child. You will feel the clarity of my essence in the tip of your nose. Breathe with me. Allow for our joint breath to be carried to every corner of that, which I AM. Keep breathing, my child. There is so much to learn about our breath. There are so many qualities to dissolve in the breath. May it become the unconditional love that I AM.

Keep breathing ...

> As it all begins

Keep breathing ...

> As it all unfolds

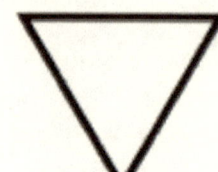

Keep breathing ...

> As it all dissolves

Keep breathing ...

> As it all becomes one

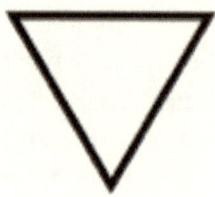

Keep breathing ...

> Inside that, which, I AM

Keep breathing ...

> We are one

Keep breathing ...

> As the heavens meets the earth

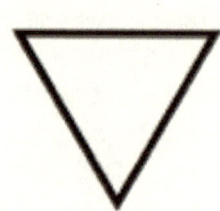

Keep breathing ...

> Until *your* heart says, it is done.

Keep breathing ...

ALONE & RESENTFUL

"This new chapter starts for me. A chapter where I am gradually given a place in the family table. I am being asked questions and I am listened to! I am so excited but what do I say? What do I want? It all feels so much more important than what I have to say. I wonder…"

"I felt alone and separate from the rest of the family but I couldn't recognise this feeling, so what do I do? What any five-year-old would do. Get into mischief! I am craving attention, I am yearning to feel connected again!

I love playing, I love being cheeky, I love smiling and I love testing boundaries. Not knowing that I am coming out from a strong traumatic experience. I was not much on the helm driving consciously. Not knowing that all the flight and fight response, of the wounding, had taken over. In its sacred duty, attempting to protect the most innocent parts of me."

"I am choosing, as life presents itself through me and for me."

In the fifth year on earth, there was a big change in the family dynamic. This year our family unit decided to move to the giant neighbouring country in the north. The country where you got *your* toys from and that spoke English. *Your* human father, also my child, was offered a big job and his corporate career had just skyrocketed. This year you saw a new world, *your* family moved to Richmond, Virginia in the USA. You were too advanced academically to be in preschool in the USA, so you were moved up to first grade. There you were immersed inside the deep program of competition. You entered the world of prices and rankings for everything where it is possible.

You were really very good at this game of competition! You won lots of prizes! You aced so much in this competitive based system that you were systematically winning prices and invited to join a school for *Special Gifted Kids* and continue to live in the USA.

This timeline was not considered by *your* bloodline. Inside *your* ancestors' truth, *your* particular bloodline didn't feel safe in this neighbouring country. It didn't feel true. *Your* family stayed together and moved back to Mexico, and thanks to these deep knowing, *your* soul was protected from the deep machinery of identity engineering up north.

Back in Mexico, you entered into *your* old school but a year advanced from *your* old kindergarten friends. You were too young to even remember them, so you moved on. Now you were the youngest and smallest inside of *your* new classroom. The wounds from being bullied by bigger boys arised. In this cycle around, you chose instead to fight and you chose to compete.

During these times, you can't understand what is happening inside of you. The unravelling of the unseen parts of you were generating feelings of resentment that started to build up and a defensive pattern of the subconscious mind had started to form.

You didn't feel safe with others and for you, feeling insecure, became the normal way of feeling. You were still too young to recognise contrasts. Competing with *your* classmates became *your* weapon. The feeling of *alone* was not recognised for you until seven years old, and the choice of feeling *resentment* was not a true and a frontal option, for you, also up until you were seven years old. Do you remember what happened then, my child?

"I do, and I am recognising more now! Towards the end of *my* seventh year, I was again at summer camp in New Hampshire, USA. This time I was alone with a *cousin*, who was not really blood related. This time *my* entire family is in Europe, and apparently the perception that I agreed to, with them, was that I was too young and mischievous to go to the sophistication of the *old world*, as Europe has been described. In truth I was simply agreeing with that perspective, because I could see that this is what they wanted, and I love them."

At seven, deep inside, you were going alone to summer camp, and all you felt was being unwanted from *your* pack; *your* family. This summer, for the first time, you felt deeply alone. You didn't ask for this and you felt a deep resentment towards *your* mother for this happening, and you buried it deep. At that time, you felt *sad and lonely* at *your* core, and you pretended that this wasn't happening. Six weeks later, back in Mexico, with *your* family, you are asked

'How are you?
　　How did you go?
　　　　What happened?'

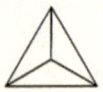

　　　　"I am good."
　　　　　"I did great."
　　　　　　"I won prizes!"

A big sense of pride and success filled the room. Did you make friends? "*Not really.*" You perceive a sense of worry in *your* mother's eyes. "I did make one friend." A sense of relief is felt in her. She asks more questions about *your* friend, you avoid them. It is not spoken of again. The next chapter continues …
　　You continue to be deeply disconnected from *your* truth. Unable to speak about what is actually happening for you in life. Suppressing this pattern of feeling alone and resentful as deep as you could. A pattern that has continued to show up in all *your* intimate relationships. A pattern that looks like *your* inability to take *rejection* or even *boundaries* well. A pattern that is

still playing out for you now, as you write these words and that you can now experience consciously.

"Are you willing to embrace alonement, my child?"

It is in being alone that *All is One* and you can only find this unity in the One that is there and then. Exactly where you are alone. All-one.

You need this alone time, my child. To feel the unity of all things in you. I truly want for you to have eternal peace in the heart. Are you willing to let go of all that breathes in you that is not love? Are you willing to love *your* mother with all of *your* heart? Are you willing to love me, with all *your* heart, as I love you? There is nothing to forgive, my child. We are one, guiding each other home.

Once you are willing to continue to express *your* most vulnerable voice. Once you are willing to simply be you and be the love that you are, no matter what. Once you are willing to surrender *your* will to I, and allow me to perform the miracles. You will find me, as you, as I AM. All that you truly desire, my child, in the depths of love, will come to be manifest in *your* life. It is up to you, my child, to choose. Every moment that you choose what is, aware of this or not, you are choosing me. I AM here offering you light into the matter.

I am here offering you my unconditional support with *your* choices. As painful as some choices can be, for us. I love you and our will as I AM will be done. You are not alone, my child. You are never alone. We will work through the matter and release the great lies that tell you that you are alone, that you are separate, and that you need protection.

There are many *man-made* programs, *advised* to you by the *tricks* of the *dark one*, who is also living in you. These mental *programs* have adhered to *your vibrations* and have been in possession of the mind in you. These programs have been creating the perception that you constantly need protection. It is this program that is saying that you can't be safe, and a complete being by *yourself*.

Now, my child, you can see the truth of this falsehood, and actually *protect* or better said, *free yourself* from what is not true. There is no need to fear the unknown. There is no need to reject what you fear. There is no need to judge what you don't understand. It is all you in this world. You are only doing this to *yourself*. Love and embrace. Fear and rejection; it is *your* choice.

You have found this undertone, of alone and resentful, playing throughout your life. Now, you know that it plays out in the underbelly when you feel rejected. Now you know that it is not really you but a program, taking you away from who you are. As the doubt arises again, now you can choose.

Are you alone? Have you ever been alone? Please see the illusion of feeling alone. My child, I am eternally here for you to remember who I AM.

If you can, please forgive *yourself* for feeling resentment towards the women that love you. Please forgive *yourself* for feeling resentment towards the beautiful feminine that lives in you. No one has left you. No one has rejected you. No one has abandoned you. There is no one to forgive, my child. Please allow for love to come in through all of you and expand *your* body and *your* expression to who you are now. Please allow for surrender to guide you to me.

Your mind is getting in the way, getting lost in finding a translation of what love is. Please allow *yourself* to be seen, felt and experienced by others. You are my child, and who experiences you in this life, is also experiencing me. The love that I AM. Please allow. I am here, very excited about our soon to be sacred union. The union of love that is happening, right now, in the occurrence of the breath inside the holy body that you are. Please allow.

The sacred union is inevitable. It is the natural state of being. It is in the allowance, my child, that you are permitting our sacred union to be. I love you, my child. Thank you for allowing for our love to be as it has always been.

"May the truth of unity be seen and felt by the many."

RELATIONSHIP WITH MEN

We are now going to share how *your* experience as a *man amongst men* started to shape you. This chapter is with the intention to unravel and dissolve the stories that tell you what a man is supposed to be and supposed to do in this world. It is clearly not working. This chapter is for you to witness the depth of the masculine wounding and its impact on *your* world. The deep untrust there is towards the masculine. We are together grieving the thousands of years of domination, deception and competition amongst each other.

"As a man I can genuinely say that we love to be apologetically straight with other men. We are also terrified of this, until we can have integrity with ourselves. As a man I can authentically share that we feel the safest when our word has integrity and it can pierce through the veil and the fabric of creation. Offering a word that offers a clear, simple, structured and open space to create from.

As men we have a lot of work to do and unravel the imposed limitations in our hearts. A good start is to examine and define our truth."

"Where am I, exactly?"

Let us examine with some questions:

How deep down are you grounded in *your* being?
Are you brain deep, throat deep, heart deep, gut deep, seed deep or are you whole, complete and free to be and have the truthful ability to respond to the moment?

Can you feel any energy stuck somewhere and not allowing you to breathe deeply?
Can you see exactly what this is?
Can you feel this without creating a story justifying or minimising this feeling?
Can you see this stuckness feeling without judging *yourself* or another person as being wrong?

Inside the world of illusions. You have been told there is a separation from the unity with our sacred mother below. This false belief in *your* inheritance has you, not only stuck inside. It has you convinced, the higher perspective is found by *walking tall, being tight and dismissive, untouched by the filth of the earth,* protected inside a *sky-rise*. This is far from the truth. I AM the higher perspective and I AM you.

It is an important practice, in getting to know yourself, walking consciously, to dissolve these unnatural frequencies from our body that do not allow you to be. Have a look and witness yourself, my child.

How are you walking?
What part of you is leading when you are walking?
What part of you is making the decisions for *your* life?
Who is walking?

Are you walking on *your* feet or are you using the illusions to feel *safe*? Are you using *your* knees or other parts of *your* body as crutches, dissociating from the earth's connection?

As you walk, observe. Where do you feel *pressure*? These pressures can be very subtle. Do you feel any *pressure* at all?

Can you describe the *who,* leading *your* life?
Who is that?
Who is talking behind these subtleties?
Who do you serve?
Have you made peace with this pain from separation?

"Let there be light."

Why do you insist on being separate from me, my child? Why do you insist on proving *yourself* to me? In fact all these stories are not allowing for you to really know how to walk on earth, with me, and with our beloved mother.

The biggest lie to ourselves, my child, is thinking that we know. Thinking that we know what, who and when is better for us. Thinking that we can pretend existence with mental images and ideas. Pretending that we are whole, complete and alive. When in fact we are hiding and operating life as a half or as quarter of a being. This is just not sustainable and it is all imploding now. Does this make sense to you, my child?

Anything that is not whole, will end up suffering, ceasing to exist. As simple as that. This is nature. We all need to be whole to be truly existing in life. A flower broken in half will die in a day or two. A tree broken in half will mostly die in a year or two. An animal broken in half will die in an hour or two. Anything that is broken will perish, soon enough. Including the soul, which still carries personality.

Love is all that you are. Just as love is all that exists. The uniqueness of form is simply the free self-expression of the elements that you are, as I AM. It is only *in-love* that you can expand *your* field to cover, embrace and embody all that we are. For this is to be in free-will and the *natural* state of being. If you are not *in love*, the natural flow of all that you are, ceases to exist. Outside of love there is a limited, narrow and tricky field, back home.

Inside this battle to feel *whole* and *complete* again, is where most of humanity is trapped. Attempting to take from others, the *thing* that seems to be what we need to feel again, for another moment, as our true selves. In this chapter you and I, my child, are going to embody the true masculine. The masculine that is a whole and complete presence of love. As I AM. This is who you are and this will never change. We will unravel together, the layers of the masculine conditioning that doesn't allow you to be all that I AM.

☥

Today my child, if you are up for it, I want us to write about *your* historical relationship with *your* own manhood. This is a very big and confusing wound that many men and women are navigating through. It will take time for us to unravel this mess. It is a wound that is covered by many layers of guilt, anger and shame. It is these wounds that have pushed men to pretend to be in strength, through controls, judgements, force and prejudice. Can you share your own experience?

"It has been very confusing. The wounded masculine in me was deeply afraid. As a teenager, seeking to be in dominant groups of men for safety. To be part of these popular groups. I needed first to earn my entry through being dominant myself. Either by using strength, money or sex.

First, I strategically dominated with my fists. I fought my way through. Then I wasn't growing much, as a teenager, and somewhat became part of the *small* crew. I had no more access to the dominant groups with my fists anymore. Except, it was then that I remembered. It is the time to share my secret experiences with feminine seduction. I am charming, I know how to talk to the opposite sex. Women feel safe with me. This is my way in!

I started then to create bonds with the good looking girls, and came into the dominant groups that way. Most of the time as a teenager, the social game of relationship building, for the future, happened inside of nightclubs and parties. I was very good in this *game*, of the art of *the deal*. I felt powerful in the dominant group. We all did. Inside these groups a lot can be accomplished and also destroyed.

The nightclub scene was, however, not a very healthy place to establish love and healthy relationships for the future. Inside this sexualised environment, many illusions and delusions happen."

You became masterfull in this *night* game, my child, and then you got over this game, you felt *cheated*. Regardless, this was long after many trials and tribulations growing up. Let us start again, where we left off, you are seven years old.

What can you share with us now?

"I am back into the embodied experience of *being Mexican*. I am almost eight years old, and I am the second smallest in the class and in a new school. Competitive ideas filled my mind, from my experience up north, and for Gods' sake: I wanted my burgers, ketchup, and I wanted my Taco Bell!

It didn't take long, and I was *Mexicanised* again.

Thankfully I am enjoying its amazing culture and cuisine. By then, I had already used my new competitive ways of being, to assert myself as the dominant boy of my class. The best at playing football. The best in class. The best with the girls. The alpha eight year old. Haha, so I thought.

Here I am, eight years old. Feeling like a king in the new school. However, after school I felt very awkward. I was being bullied in the local football team. I loved football so much but one day I arrived at home, after practice, and I told mom and dad. "I am not playing football anymore." 'What!? Why!?' "I don't like it anymore, it is boring." This did not make sense to them. I loved football. They keep asking questions just to find out that I really don't want to go because I was being bullied by a pack, and this pack included an adult!

Soon enough, my dad, furious, comes to practice, confronts the adult, and gives me the green light to fight each one of these boys, right then and there. I do, and I regain security and respect from the rest of the team. Yet, I have crossed this sacred line. I am now not afraid of fighting with my fists. I am not afraid of physicaly punching, hurting and dominating others to be *respected*. It seems to work."

This is how it started, my child. You have been fighting and dominating men all *your* life. In truth, you have been afraid of them. You are not alone, my child. This is an epidemic amongst men. Men need to learn to trust men again.

You continued to fight and you continued to charm *your* way through. Getting expelled from two schools. Creating many friends and creating some enemies. Inside of you, justifying the actions with one simple statement: 'This is how the game works.'

For this story in particular, my child. As a teenager and young adult, you felt as if you could do anything. A dominant group of friends formed in high-school, nicknamed *the scarabs* and became quite present to the teenage social scene of Mexico City. Inside of a particular moment of a deep social vacuum for identity in the country. The charm and confidence of this group was felt. Amongst you, the group had high level economic, industrial, political and social influence. Inside a particular time in this country, where the power spectrum was very centralised. You felt like royalty. You witnessed how this culture spread to other groups, and you felt how being part of this group opened a big window of opportunities. Fast forward to now, my child, and you can recognise how all these *dominant* moments took you out of *your* body and numbed *your* sensitivity. You started to break sacred values and block the ease of sacred energy within. This severed *your* connection with our mother earth and with all that you are.

How deep is the damage?

"As men, we are enduring enormous damage to our sacredness. We have severed the pure characteristics of a mans' love. Now, it is in remembering, acknowledging and particularly in the grieving that we can come back to our purity as men."

We are, dear one, in the source of all beings, made from love. We all come from Love. Even if you are a *non-believer*. Limited to physical phenomena. Our parents making love, made us. Saying this, how is the love of the masculine distinct from the love of the feminine. A pure masculine's love, is a love that is present and crystal. A love that is expansive, from the centre. A love that is firm and still. A love that is gentle and surrendered to what is right in front of them. A love that can see the fabric of creation. A love that remembers eternity. A love that pierces through the fabric of form, and a love that forgives all that is not love in them.

      Inside the peace of presence. Is what a true man feels like. Where are you unclear, unstable or stuck as a man, my child,? Let's do this transformation together! Not only for a fleeting moment or a fleeting breath but inside of every moment and every breath.

"May men, in the many, return back to the source of power, beauty and love."

"I am a man that is unsure on how to embody all of myself. It appears that without the presence of another, with whom I have a heart connection, I don't know how to be embodied."

I am aware of this, my child. It is true in the eternal now for the many. This is not true for you, as you write, yet it will be true for you later in the journey, when the vastness of space and time brings doubt into *your* psyche. Much of this remembrance is for *your* integration as you share, and to open the healing for the many.

"Today, in truth, I am unsure of my path, and of *my* offering for this world. I am writing from the beginning of the journey, in the intention to give clarity to *myself* as a man amongst men. Dedicating this work to all men who are seeking, and to all men who are living as fully connected, breathing and sensing human beings."

As men, it requires precision, clarity of context, structure and integrity for our efforts to be aligned with the blossoming of the love that we are inside. Our love, as men, breaks through the fabric and creates a clear space for our feminine love, inside, to manifest. The fabric that creates the continuous energy in motion and cosmic dance. The fabric that keeps us conditioned into some form. The fabric where the stories of humanity are being weaved together.

To break through, back into nothing, is a key role of the masculine within. Asserting the qualities of presence and integrity to the word that speaks. This Is asserting the power of creator, architect and builder, as I AM. This is essentially and existentially, important to the masculine. This, my child, is as important to me, as it is to you.

How can this power be available for you. For me, and available for all men and women? How can this be?

"'We must compete amongst ourselves!" - Concludes the doubting of a scared man.

Where does this doubt come from, my child? Please don't go anywhere. What are you afraid of? Let's do this together. What is confusing?

"I am at the cusp of my personal development in this lifetime. I feel strong, solid, clear, and reliant. Yet, I feel doubtful, small, hard and frustrated. More than ever. I don't want to make a mistake. I don't want to be alone. How can this be?"

It is my child. This is what it is to be human. Can you observe that it is *yourself*, who is observing all of this? It is you who is serving as a container for all of these polarised feelings to exist, together with all the thoughts that are attached to them.

"It is you who we are liberating, through the journey in the form of this book."

Let's take this back down a layer, my child. You have been witnessing a doubtful and punished man existing within you. You have been dealing with tightness and heaviness in *your* shoulders, back and neck. This is very common amongst the masculine. You have taken on the burden of power, instead of harnessing and channelling the infinite energy within for the service of creation.

You have allowed for a strict punisher to promote the discipline that is actually gained through practice and repetition. The masculine in you, and in many, has misunderstood the fabric. It has collapsed a feeling of burden when responsibility is present, and it has collapsed a feeling of strictness when discipline is present.

This is very common, my child. The masculine has lost touch of the feminine within and has been out of centre. It has lost access to the nurturing wisdom of the feminine that allows us to have the peaceful space to be inside. A man that has learnt to survive with a disconnection from the feminine is a man that is seeking outside. Seeking nurture and love in the form of women, food, things and substances. Holding an anxious heart, seeking outside for *the one* that has always been exactly where you are. This is very common, my child, amongst men. Can you observe all of the feelings that you might have right now?

"Frustration from unfulfilled dreams. Despair from not being where I want to be and not having the power to change it. Anxiety from feeling that I am running out of time."

What is below that, my child?

"A seed that wants to create life. A seed that is afraid of being alone and is seeking connection. A seed of life that feels surrounded by pain and anxiety."

This is beautiful my child and yet the biggest drain of *your* vital energy. You are seeking the wholeness of connection and unconditional love outside of you. This is creating the forgetfulness that you are this love *yourself*. You are forgetting that you are never alone, as you are *all one*. You are forgetting who you truly are.

"The One and Only."

Do you remember where you come from?
Do you remember why you are here?
Do you remember where you are going?

It is perfect to not have answers, my child. We are going to remember together. Looking outside is why we get lost, dear one. For us to remember, and fully embody the truth that you are, there is a lot of de-programming and reprogramming that is needed for you.

The world that you live in is not *your* ally, unless you make it so. It is perfectly designed to show you all that is and all that isn't. It is designed to confuse you and to create the forgetfulness of who you are, dear child. In the world where you are, there are so many layers of identity that force you to pigeon-hole each other, into the fragmentation of a role and demographics.

The world that you live in is full of human beings, pretending to be in power. Pretending that it is all glamorous and fun. Pretending that they think they know. Speaking from a place of control and pretending that everything in their life is in perfect order. It is all pretend, my child. All these untruths are compounded, everywhere you look. This is why *your* world is so confusing to the soul that you are. Creating a constant view of comparison and division that is continuously pushing you out of the divine presence within.

You are not alone, my child. Let's keep remembering.

We will go a step at a time, through the fabric within, take *your* time to reflect, feel and transcend.

"It is in the one, in who you are, that all becomes one."

☥

My child, continue to work with me. We can let go of this want for external love and you can be at peace, inside with me. Resting in *your* own love. Resting in *your* heart. Resting in the love that I AM.

It is when you are able to choose me as *your* eternal beloved that it all transforms and blessings pour down in *your* life, dear one. This union, as everything else, will also fleet away. It will be gone, again, the moment that *your* mind is occupied seeking for a purpose outside. It happens every time. Do *your* current actions satisfy the depth of *your* soul? Are *your* depths satisfied with what you are choosing to do in life? These are the questions to be clear about. You cease to exist, in *your* core, when you are out of *your* existential desire to be one with me, as I AM.

I am in spirit, and as you are, I AM. All in divine timing, my eternally beloved child. You are healing *your* seed. Sitting with the uncomfortable feeling of *your* own sexual anxieties. All the unhealthy erotic stories that you fantasised, suppressed or got corrupted with, are being met. All of the stories that were not part of the grace of creation but made into existence from *your* own forceful and disconnected imagination and disconnected flesh. Not really connected to the harmony of nature.

It is great to feel desire, my child. Acknowledging *your* desire is how you live *full heartedly*. A healthy relationship, that creates with me, happens when there is a full-heart inside sacred reciprocity.

All those years of finding *your* manhood through the conquest of women. All those years, seeking connection. You played with the fire of creation, my child, and you got burnt. You didn't know how to use this sacred fire for *your* own healing, and were simply giving it away or building up frustration that would then explode and destroy *something* that you love.

Where are you feeling lost, my child?

"I am lost in the images of doing. Lost in the roles I need to play. Lost in comparing myself with others. Lost in the worry of survival. Lost in the ups and downs of emotions and medicines. I understand that all this suffering is of my own doing."

Take a breath, my child. I love you. Please trust in me as *your* provider and creator. There is no need to use *your* force when you trust in my divine power. Learn to live connected with me and our creation. Together, you will be at ease receiving grace. As the outside is only a reflection of *your* inside, my child.

Essentially, you didn't know how to breathe into the love that I AM and be one with *yourself*. You didn't know how to love unconditionally. You didn't know how to be with the feminine in truth. You didn't know how to receive another with vulnerability. Now my child, you know how and you can sit with the uncomfortable anxiety and rejoice in all that you are.

Keep doing this work, my child. You will soon enough start feeling the layers fading away into their liberation. You will soon have a deeper and rooted space available to host you, the love that I AM. Keep doing this work, my child, please be patient as I AM. Breath into this. I am eternally patient and I understand *your* feelings right now. Maybe *your* father and mother, in the human world, were not very patient with you, my child. Maybe this message can be confusing to *your* feelings.

Please, if you so desire dear one, be as I AM. To see *yourself* as I AM, you do need to let go of *your* human identities. Including *your* family and culture so you can walk with me in Spirit. Walk with who is eternally in you. This journey is the definition of the divine masculine within. The definition of heaven on earth. This is the process when you empty *your* home from all external identification. To freely choose *your* embodiment and manifestation on earth. Allowing you to choose the embodiment of what is divine, what is true, and what is beautiful.

"I really want to be with you! There is all this noise that doesn't allow me to be at peace within you. I am angry and scared at my fellow men. I don't trust their intentions. I don't trust my intentions. I don't trust men to speak in truth and to look after the vulnerability that is sacred for women and children. I don't trust myself deep inside as well. For the sake of the children, men, we need to hold ourselves with integrity. I am using plant medicines to find peace in my heart, and I am using them too much. This doesn't allow me to be fully centred and embodied in I AM. I am losing the magnetic power that I AM by entertaining myself too much with plant medicines."

My child, one day at a time. We will breathe together and start dissolving all that doesn't allow us to be together. We will breathe together so you can let go of *your* substance addictions, and we will continue to practise forgiveness towards *yourself* and *your* fellow men.

Please stop my child. Please stop destroying *yourself* with judgement. We are all in this together. Forgiveness for all the falsehoods and for all the destruction that men, like you, have created throughout history. All in the search for power that I AM. Destruction of core values, destruction of the sacred, destruction of *your* vitality. All of this destruction seeking the power that I AM.

"I have been hurting myself, being hard on myself, not recognising the gentle being that I am. Not recognising the infinite power that resides inside the gentle laws of nature.

I am sorry to myself. I am sorry to you."

There is nothing to forgive, my child. What are you, as a man, going to make happen? What do you choose?

"I choose to be a vessel for heaven's timeline on earth."

What does heaven on earth look like, my child?

"I am living in harmony, in community with nature, abundantly in all possible ways and sharing this with the people that I love the most. Spirit is tangible and present, guiding us."

I hear you. These are beautiful dreams that we share, my child. The vessel, looks in you as I AM.

Please take these messages with you:

- A surrendered vulnerable and powerful human, is true to themselves and others.

- A human that is true doesn't see failure but every moment as an opportunity for purposeful action to transform life.

- A human, in truth, uses free time, not for distraction but for feeling the deepest available uncomfortable *wounds* and finds pleasure and joy in doing so.

- A true human, my child, walks gently on earth, speaks with an open heart, connects with ease, and stands firmly, breathing deeply, in the truth of the sacred.

☥

"I am perfectly blessed. I am as my heavenly father and my sacred mother created me. I am here to serve you as I am. I am here to continue to recognise the big mess the wounded boy inside of me created, while I have been pretending to be a man.

In all honesty, I have been using all the archetypes at my disposal: My dad, my brothers, my friends, the wizard, the warrior, the king, the lover to keep hiding the most vulnerable truth that I AM. Speaking like everybody else. Fitting into a mental construct of what it means to be a man.

Pretending to be good. Pretending to have everything under control. Pretending that a man is only here to provide and protect. I have been empty in love. Yet giving a big and generous love to others. Pretending to be healthy. In fact I have been hurting myself, and the people in my sphere of influence."

I know, my child, that in this present moment you don't want to write this book anymore. I know that you are doubting *your* seed. I know that you are seeking, instead, for new life experiences in this reality of matter.
Trust the matter, as the matter is also you. The matter is there to help you feel and see the depths that come from the contrasts and from the suffering of separation.
If you are called to be with the matter, that is where you are called to be. The matter is empowering and

enriching, when we learn its laws and trust what is in front of us. It is constricting and confusing, when we do not understand the rules. The matter becomes blissful as we embody our natural law. Our natural law is love. You know this, my child.

You have spent months in nature. You have seen the phenomenon of love many times. You have heard our beloved mother speak to you. 'Break down those walls, my child!' The spirit of the great mother is indeed shouting at us. 'Break down those walls!'
The divine feminine in this world stops men in our tracks: 'Stop pretending!'

I surrender
I continue to surrender
I AM

I know nothing	I know nothing
I am that I am	I am That I am
I breath that I am	I breath that I am
I AM	I AM

'Stop pretending' The divine feminine within me continues to shout.

"How deep does this *pretending* go? When will I actually allow myself to be? I am so unfamiliar with the masculine authentic self. I am not sure what a true masculine looks and feels like. How can I stop pretending?"

You are not alone, my child. There have not been many

examples of the divine masculine on earth, outside of the tales that you have received from religion.

"Inside this moment, now, I am alone again, getting to know the masculine that I am. I feel unsafe in my legs and at the same time, I feel contained. Below my belly button, I feel sexual doubts of not being attractive enough. I feel doubt in my will power, am I good enough. A couple of fingers below my rib cage, I feel anger and frustration within that space. The warrior within shouts back at me 'you are good enough!' I feel on top of that a heart that is unsettled, wanting to create beauty for this world. I feel a deep voice that wants to roar against all the lies and injustices in this world. I feel focus and determination. I observe a mind that is clouded in time and space, from all the pondering and from a continuous addiction with plant medicine."

Yes, my child! What was once a medicine for you, now has become a poison. Together, we will breathe out from these doubts and addictions. For now you need to focus on *your* immediate needs and build *your* discipline there.

I will guide you through this process. Are you willing to continue to let go of *your* desire towards the feminine's flesh and the vanity that you blemish in? "I am." You are beautiful, my child. *Your* presence is sought by many. Please forgive *yourself* for the past.

Your energy is and, as it is, it will create its' designed impact on earth. You are doing it, as you write the truth that I AM. *Your* commitment will make it so.

It is by having the discipline of being a student, learning in every moment, that will open the gates of where you want to be. Are you willing to have discipline in your life? To integrate mastery, you first have to learn how to be a disciple. The master becomes when she or he learns how to always be a student.

I love you, my child. It doesn't matter how you feel in the mornings, afternoons and evenings. We are in this together. A man becomes a man with discipline, and men come together, when there is a clear goal.

You are the biggest goal there is. You are the canvas, the artist and the paint. Daily habits and disciplines build the foundation to the masterpiece that I AM. May you keep walking, dear one, as you are. May you have clear goals for *yourself*. Goals that are clear, yet goals that are daily surrendered back to me. This way I can do the hard work for you, and you can focus on what really matters to you that is right in front of you.

What are *your* goals right now, my child?

"To be *your* victory as I AM. To finish and distribute this book. To strengthen this healthy body. To create a family and a home. To create a community."

What are you doing to achieve these goals, dear one?

"I am writing this book daily. I am slowly building my inner strength. Supporting *my* back with the earth. I am discerning the energy that I allow in, and discerning what comes out of this body. I am training and practising to remain in the centre of this being. Regardless of what is happening, in that moment. I am openly sharing myself and my goals."

What is stopping you, dear beloved?

"At times, I have been feeling powerless. Inside this despair, I can see how the energy within is wanting to go out of me and cling to the outer. Desperately looking for a saviour. Looking to show up in strength, using the engineered power of the masculine archetypes to show up and be seen. The same role models that are coming from ancestors and current leaders.

In a more direct way for me, I can see dad's righteous way showing up. Followed by moments from the virtuosity of siblings, the knowing ways of mentors, the supporting ways of dear friends, the protecting ways of wounded boys and the loving ways of soulmates. I can see that the identity of men has been pigeonholed. I can see that most men are trapped inside these *archetypes*. I can see most men needing to hold an image or an agenda, so we can make sure, in the delusion, that we are real."

This pondering sparks a deep question inside, the archetype of *my* inner child: - "Father, do I still choose Yeshua (Jesus) as my teacher and saviour?"

As you need him, my child...

As Shiva attained pure consciousness surrendering to the force of the mother, through stillness and presence, transcending the fabric of nature. Yeshua, as pure consciousness, attuned, in full surrender, to the deeper unconditional love. Above and below, as I AM.

Innocent, Playful and Eternally loving. Jeshua attained *Christendom*. Just as *Krishna*, inside its own language. As *Christ*, in this innocent state of unity, you can witness the sacred, ever present, song of unconditional love.

As this, Jesus can be in communion with you as father, as brother, as teacher, as role model, as God. You can choose my child. Yeshua is eternal. He has transcended all the matters that you are going through. Jesus is ONE with me and then again, from *your* eternal centre, he is also an archetype to free *yourself* from. Don't forget his own message, my child, 'do not look at me but follow where my finger is pointing towards.' Follow him back home, to the centre of centres, where I AM.

"I also desire deeply to be one with you father, exactly as I AM."

What do you choose, my child?
I am testing the integrity of *your* words. They will be tested in every moment and in every day. May you be one with me, exactly as you are.

"The pervasive need of being right."

Can you see the uncomfortable need to *be right* that you are facing right now, my child? Can you see *yourself* trying to find different angles of existence to invalidate *yourself*, invalidate me, and invalidate all that you are writing here as I AM.

It is great that you haven't fully chosen me, dear child. You are still finding *your* own singular truth and this is how greatness is to be manifested.

Nonetheless, I am here and I love you with all the love that I AM. I can see you finding *your* way back home, as everyone else. I can see a part of you, still looking outwards for life's essence. What are you looking for, dear beloved?

"I am looking to prove myself, constantly proving myself. But who am I proving myself to? I don't even know anymore. I do not know what it is that I am looking for."

Can I say, my child, that you have been looking for love?

    "Yes! I have been looking for the woman that I am to marry and fall in love with."

That is not it, my child. You have been looking for *yourself*! You are love, and you will always be loved, my child. This will never change, you are eternally in love!

    "Why is it then that I cannot feel this? Why do I feel so much doubt inside of me? Why do I feel so much anger, loathing and regret?"

Continue revealing and feeling, my child. You are doing great. Inside of *your* clear intention and attention to heal, it will all fade away.

    "I have been feeling a lot. Deep inside I can hear pervasive voices telling me that I am not good enough, and then I am showing completely the opposite to the world. - Deep inside I feel small and on the outside, I counteract this by creating an emboldened and charismatic persona to speak from."

You are not alone, dear one. Most men have these same self-depreciation voices inside. Most men counteract these deep insecure emotions with big and fierce personalities. Numbing and disconnecting themselves, from the moment, with future actions and distractions. As a result, most men are not embodied and are simply living a simulation of ideas created by the mind. Most men are pretending to be men. This is what has been creating the destructive culture that now most of you, my children, are a part of.

"I am still dealing with many righteous ways of being. Thinking that I am better than others. Proving all the reasons why I am right and they are not. I am more able, more informed, more intelligent, more…"

Dear child, these righteous ways come from the experience of the ancestors before you. It has birthed itself from the thousands of years of judgement. The same judgement that mankind has created when there is something different to themselves that cannot be understood.

It is these righteous ways that bring forth animosity and conflict between men. If you think about it, have you ever met anyone who likes to be wrong? Have you ever met anyone who likes to be judged? Take writing this book as an example, dear one. What are you experiencing?

"Instead of being at ease sharing all the beauty that I can see and that I can remember. I can feel a harsh, yet subtle, judgement coming from my memory and discernment. I can feel a deep fear of not wanting to be judged by writing this book. This fear then takes me out of my true vulnerability, and I start to write from an emboldened and *mightier than thou* persona. This then gives me a sense of feeling secure, yet disconnected from the vulnerable truth that I AM and therefore, disconnecting from the truth of the reader."

Thank you, my child. It is exactly this dynamic, of pretending strength, that repeats itself throughout mens' society. It brings forth a reality that is disconnected from the vulnerable truth and the natural harmony that it provides us. I purposely say that this is *men's* society, as it is men who have created the agreements of society that are now expiring for most of you.

So many convenient agreements to suppress feelings and emotions. To be *strong and independent*. To become separated from ourselves, from each other and from truth. These are the agreements that have forced wise women from the past, to cast spells over the power of men, and thus have created modern generations of emasculated men. In these times, we are getting used to men being emasculated. This has allowed for women and children to feel superficially safe but this safety is only surface deep.

The deep presence of men is needed for this safety to be felt in the core. Men are called to show up again as new, deeply committed with creation. To show up with an open heart and offer a crystal clear space for the birth of the *New Earth*. Speaking to us through the womb. It is not until men can offer a safe space for the heart, that women can feel safe in their bodies to surrender into their wombs, listening to the guidance of our mother.

Having shared this existential context of our times, are men ready to accept their true power that comes with responsibility, accountability, integrity and congruence? I do not know how this will go, my child. In the stars and in the heavens there are many stakeholders to earth being very attentive to *your* choices.

Mankind is evolving very quickly. It is up to every single one of you, men, to say yes to the truth within and learn how to surrender to the feminine inside each one of you. For this purpose, men are called, by creation, to look inside and to not leave any stone unturned. Men are called to bring congruence to thoughts, words and actions. Men are called to ensure that the whole is built and held with complete integrity. Men are called to show up with the ability to respond. Men are called to hold each other accountable. Everyday is a test. Most relevant to our times, men are called to build compassion for each other.

We are all doing our best. We are all dealing with thousands of years of oppression to the magic within. We are all dealing with thousands of years of hurting the magic from the womb. "What is inside?" you might ask.

The wounded child is all that is in the depth of *your* being. All that you do not want to see, is just that, the child that you are, asking for love and attention. It is the false belief systems, on earth, that have morphed this simplicity, to trick you to think that it is a scary demon or a complicated *medical* explanation. All the interfering noise telling you that you are separate from the pain of mankind.

Below, all the illusions of men, all you will find, which separates us, is the wounded child that wants to be seen and loved in truth. Loved unconditionally as I AM with all that I AM. You, as all that is on earth, have the qualities of the Heavenly Father that I AM. The qualities of innocence, curiosity and unity in heart with all that is. The qualities of light that are infinite, ever present and free. As well, you, as all that exists on earth, have the qualities of the Mother that I AM. The qualities of resilience, growth and primal instincts. The qualities of knowing the matter, and of knowing the unknown.

The holy child from heaven and the wild man from earth are meant to be the best of friends, dear one. Supporting, guiding and protecting each other in union.

On the other hand, we live in a society orchestrated by the fearful mind aiming to protect us. A reality where the wild man has been shamed into a cage. Containing its true power, for the safety of women and children. Where the holy child has been punished and shamed for being vulnerable and playful. Taking away the clear light of guidance that resides in the heart of men.

You see my child, all of these agreements are fuelled by fear, and this is core to the matter of the times that you are in. As the sacred womb of women, the heart of men is an essential portal for the fabrics of creation to manifest into existence.

The heart of men is sacred, and both men and women should approach it as such. It holds the keys to unveiling the sacred matter of time and space. It holds the light to see the deep secrets of the sacred womb, guiding us to the greener pastures in time.

We are in very exciting times, dear one. All of this *matter* is rapidly changing, the unveiling is happening and many of you are preparing for it. Are you ready? You are my child, I speak to you who are still doubting that I AM. Are you ready?

Thank you, dear one. This integration of the higher and the lower realms, represented as the holy child and the wild one, is how we start to bring our worlds together. This is how your heart starts to feel the safety and grounding that it yearns for. This is how you can offer the same safety to women and children in your life.

You don't have to do anything. Simply show up. The vibrations that offer this core safety are already alive in you. It is already felt by those who yearn for such a deep presence. Allow, dear beloved. We are in this together.

Allow for the fire of the earth to fuel you,
Allow for the fierce guardian of earth to surface.

Allow for the *Golden Child* to feel the protection of the *Wild One* that I AM.
Open *your* heart, my child.
The one that I AM wants to surface.

Allow, my child. Allow.

"I feel safe as I AM.
The WILD ONE is peaceful, full of instinct and protects me. I Embrace him completely.
I AM safe."

The child on earth wants to cry.
It wants to be held.
It wants to be seen.
The child knows the way.

The *child* is joyful, and feels safe on the shoulders of the *wild one* below.
The *wild one* is satisfied in its role of protecting the eternal child of love and light.

🎶 *I AM the light of the soul,*
I AM beautiful,
I AM bountiful.
This I AM, I AM, I AM 🎶

92

RELATIONSHIP WITH WOMEN

Your relationship with women has not been easy for you, dear child. Continuously giving your power away. Following and yearning the sweet and soft energy of women. Wanting to receive their love to feel loved, and seeking to feel validated as a man with their approval. Feeling a continuously present desire for women's curves and flesh.

However, underneath all of this desire and dependency, *your* subconscious has also been experiencing a deep untrust towards anything to do with women. This has been *your* journey, my child. You are not alone. This is how creation has been created to be.

Please don't judge *yourself* my child, It is perfect as it is. Most men on this planet face the same distortions. We are facing centuries of fear, bestiality and excessive force that need to be acknowledged. For many centuries there was no limit to what a man could do to a woman.

At the same time, this started to change over the centuries, through women handling and manipulating mens' hearts for a sense of control and safety for them. Doing this has created a lot of confusion and disempowerment in many men. In fact, the mess that we have on earth, can be greatly attributed to men not receiving, for centuries, true initiations to become men. Leaving women and children not feeling a true existential safety around them.

I hope that you are listening, my child. As a result of this mess, we have wounded boys and teenagers in power, pretending to be men. A wounded boy is reactive, forceful and dominating. A wounded boy in a man's body doesn't know how to offer women a safe place without a cage of walls, guards and riches. A wounded boy lives inside every single one of us, men and women, leaving us yearning inside for the healthy masculine to show up. This so we can feel whole, supported, purposeful and safe in the depths of creation.

Can we go deeper into *your* wounding, my child? You are not alone dear one. As you share *your* intimate self, others can see themselves further down their truth.

After being activated and corrupted by the *swimming teacher*, you have memories of being aroused as a small child with mature women carrying you next to their bodies. You have memories of playing with girls and playing with boys *your* age. You can feel in *your* body the deep desire to feel the pleasure that you once felt. Not understanding of the poison that was growing inside *your* body. Attacking, from the inside, the love that you are.

Then there was a shock to *your* system at about

nine years of age, where you felt like the worst human by submitting a boy to *your* sexual energy. You did this simply because it was the way for you to submit him to *your* will at the time. He was bigger in size than you and you didn't feel safe around him. I remember after the fact, in *your* own space, in his toilet. How all of your buried emotions piled up on you. The feelings were so strong that *your* mind cursed yourself out of this place of truth. You then created a command that dictated *your* life for decades, you said to *yourself*:

"I am an unwanted piece of shit."

This is precisely what you told *yourself*. This is the disempowering context that has been sitting deep in *your* subconscious, unattended, dictating many outcomes in *your* life. Now you can see dear child, now you can feel the pain of despair that is in the undertone of *your* being. Now you are healing.

This command left you navigating *your* desires, *your* spite and untrust, while navigating, at the same time, *your* deep love towards the feminine. Feeling powerless deep inside. All you had left in *your* self esteem, and self trust, when relating to women, was to reject them or to place women on a pedestal. High on a cloud so you couldn't hurt them.

In truth, where you are, as the creator, that I AM. You haven't trusted *yourself*, beloved child. *Your* own feminine. *Your* own sensual desires. *Your* own intentions inside intimate connections. Stemming from *your* own lust, *your* own unhinged appetite for flesh, and from centuries of shame and prejudice that have been suppressing *your* own innocent exploration and self realisation.

It is all perfect, dear one. It was wise to not trust *yourself* then. A fully activated *kundalini*, in a dark subconscious reality, and without any distinguished pattern that *your* mind could recognise.

    All *your* sacred sexual energy flowed strongly in *your* body, without any presence containing this force. All this creative impetus without any tools or awareness to harness, contain or direct this primal energy. It wasn't easy for you. I feel you and I love you for this journey. You are a true warrior of love, willing to bring it all out to light and to be witnessed by many. A warrior of love, as I AM, choosing to recognise, surrender and heal the deep wounds inside of creation. *Your* healing is my healing.

From this Godhead perspective you are great, pure and beautiful, my child, and you have always been great, pure and beautiful. You are experiencing the depth of *your* existential vessel with love and humility. You are now surrendering to the moment with women and men around you in presence, strength and vulnerability. This is a very powerful choice, dear child.

It takes a lot to do what you are doing. I am so proud of you. After that time, of disconnecting with the feminine love within you, you took shelter behind sports and you played football like a dream. You were so good at this sport. All *your* vital energy was being used and you were so happy being a leader in *your* team, and excelling in this sport.

This emotional bypass came with a toll though. As *your* peers grew into puberty they were coupling up and you were simply too scared and overwhelmed with the feminine energy to engage. This now created another trauma, a common teenage wound of not belonging and not being good enough, in comparison with others, to be loved. This sparked and awoke the dormant beast inside. You were not going to be left behind in this quest of teenagers to couple up and start to discover sexual energy. You felt ahead from the pack and you were determined to show *your* peers *your* super powers and be admired by them. It is fair to say that this plan totally failed! You were simply too scared and overwhelmed to approach the girls you liked.

This inaction simply made the story of not being good enough stronger. This was a blow to *your* self esteem. In this place of lack you decided that you were going to focus on the girls you didn't like and simply use them to satisfy *your* needs. This went for over a decade. Woman after woman. You only knew the transaction of using each other. Using them to feel as a man, using them to be accepted into the *cool* groups, using them to satisfy *your* urges but you are not alone, dear child. You were also used, please forgive *yourself* and please forgive all *your* brothers and sisters for using each other.

You chose to be *handsome*, to the times. You chose to be a strong being. You chose a big heart. You chose to be sensitive. You chose intelligence. You chose a strong character. You chose charisma. You chose social status. Can you see that you were also used by women in *your* life? and it is perfect as it is.

It is ok to accept that humans mostly use each other. Authentic relating, inside of unconditional love, is very rare on earth. Especially amongst teenagers where it all seems to be moving so fast, and yet so slow and confusing.

Even now, inside the conscious and present loving container that you share with a beloved. You are both in the present moment finding out that you are still using each other, for something. For *your* own greater good. You are seeing that you need to let each other go as the purity of unconditional love is still not there for you and her. You have transformed and you continue to transform to be more as I AM, thank you dear one.

Inside this new paradigm of being, you are now vulnerably surrendered to connecting with life. You are listening deeply and you continue to open up to receive more love. In the now, you are attracting beautiful, empowered and embodied holy women. In the now moments, you are truly and authentically dealing with the, so called, *stuff* that would stop you from shining through. You are driven, you are whole, you are holy: "I AM." What do you need to forgive my child to let go of *your* guilt with women?

"I need to let go of desire, I keep seeing their bodies as sources of desire. I am tired and ashamed. Father, how can I create this transformation?"

Nothing to be ashamed of, my child. It is the fuel of vitality that you seek. The source of creation.

You are this vitality and you are the source of this creation. In truth you are still not connecting with me as *your* source, inside of every moment. You see dear beloved, you keep looking outside for love and you haven't yet come back full circle. You haven't yet harnessed all of *your* energy back home, to feel *your* own love and true eternal existence. Please continue to do nothing and to give, in *your* breathing and in *your* silence, all of this sacred love to *yourself* that I AM. You are dealing with centuries of programming that are telling you that the woman that you conquer is what makes you a man. You, as countless men here, seek women for validation, worthiness and love. Men, you are not alone. Women also seek men to validate themselves as beautiful and worthy.

Below all, this web of lies that have orchestrated human *reality*. Underneath all of it, we look to the feminine for softening and to validate our inner feelings of love and eternity. On the other hand, women look to the masculine to strengthen the spine and to strengthen their own confidence inside the physical world on Earth.

You were told many lies, dear child. In the core of this web of falsehoods, you were told that being a man means to have power to control *your* environment. This is a core lie to the essence of existence, and directly impacts where you are.

You see, firstly, you are my child. Therefore you are all the power that is and will ever exist. Then you can't truly have or possess something that is already inherently who you are.

Secondly, you can't control anything outside of you. Even-though, for a temporary moment you might think otherwise. All the life outside of you, has also been created through their own birthright of *free will*.

Lastly, you are the environment and the environment is you. The environment, like *anything* else, wants to be listened to, acknowledged and honoured. The environment wants to connect with you, so you can truly know what you both need to prosper.

Can you see the dear one? Have you been able to figure *yourself* out yet? It is *all* inside of you. You are it. Everything that you see in *your* life is a reflection of what is inside of you, and it only wants to be seen and recognised to exist and evolve. You are all living inside a paradox of reflections.

Through time you are the Alpha and you are the Omega. In space, like me, you can be anywhere at once. You are the inner and the outer. The higher and the lower. You are, as I AM.

The energy that is generated in any moment inside of you, is equivalent to more power than that of all nuclear weapons that are right now on earth. How can you possibly be looking for any-*thing* outside of you, dear child? How can you possibly believe that some-*thing* outside will be more gratifying than the eternal and infinite love that you can spring and give to *yourself*? It is only the mind telling you otherwise.

Honour, respect and protect this body that you are, dear one. This body, that you are, is the highest technology on earth! There is so much for you to still learn from the body, dear beloved. *Your* vessel to communicate, manifest, transport, alchemise and transcend.

The body, my child, can be used as your transport, *your* communication device, *your* healing companion and *your* source of energy. The technology inside of the body is the truth of the source of *your* power. This is of great importance to you, and somehow this message is not reaching many of my children.

There is a systematic force in *your world*, that I have allowed to play, that doesn't want you to know this. This force, disconnected from its source, attempts to control, to feel security and power. It doesn't want you to know that all of creation, past, present and future, and all of its wisdom, power and technology lives inside of you.

I have empowered this one, and other channels to communicate light and counteract this shadow. It is all perfect, dear one, it is evolving in the divine timing of what is possible. Expand the body with *your* voice. Open *your* voice and use it to honour *your* body. When your soul sings the whole universe can hear you. Learn the laws of *your* land so you can navigate the machinery that is against and for you. It is all made in spirit. Learn about the technology of the body, make your body vibrate, this ancient wisdom has never left Earth.

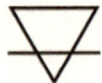

I hear you, my child. Doubt is still present.

"What about my addiction to gain the attention and the affection from women?"

This is the matter that you want freedom from the most, dear one. You see, at the deepest core of *your* navel, you have been separated from *your* mother. Even before birth, before *your* conception and even before being a possible dream to *your* ancestors.

My beloved, covert and perverse plans, from the deceitful one that is also alive in you, has separated you from *your* mother. The ancient connection with *your* own mother has not been passed on to you. You are not connecting with her wisdom, support and nurture in *your* depths. It is in the body that we can connect with her.

You are not alone, my child! The ways of the mother have not been passed on to modern humans for hundreds of years. The initiations coming from the five elements are not part of modern humanity anymore, and humanity is pretending to exist without this natural force and unconditional love. All that comes from mother earth, and that runs like water through our own bones and veins. This is the core of *your* unsustainability as humanity. This is the core of the anxiety that makes many of you into consuming machines. This disconnection, with the mother, is manifesting in you as despair, and *your* mother is shedding, in her own way, that her children are disconnected and afraid.

This lack of connection with the earth and its essence within the body only brings despair. It creates a separation from the soft and gentle nurture that comes to any being that is truly walking on earth. It creates resistance and a disconnection from the wild force of nature that lives within. It is truly daunting to exist without this connection. The message to you my child, the one listening, cannot be stronger.

Walk barefoot on earth.
Rest your back on trees.
Secure land.
Come together in community.

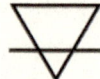

Further to these suggestions, my child. I am going to be very direct with you right now and remind us of something before we finish this chapter. Being aware or knowing about *your* sexual past, doesn't make a difference to *your* quality of life and in fulfilling *your* deepest desire of healing and becoming one as I am with our sacred father and mother inside of one.

Do you *get* this? Knowing really doesn't make a difference. You can only get it as you go through it.
It is inside of *it* that we can see, feel, forgive and release. It is only *through it* that we *get it*.

How much do you want to be free from these

ancestral and collective wounds, dear one? Do you really want to do this?

    "Yes"
Yes, are you sure?
    "Yes"

Ok then, you have agreed to continue in this journey. I am confirming with you that you truly want to do this child. We are going to feel the depths of *your* uncomfortability with the feminine within you.
    We will feel together. The root of these sexual anxieties. Let's do it now so more can see themselves in their depths. Find your quiet stillness, dear one

Right now, what do you feel immediately in *your* body?
    "I feel shame in my chest and heart."
What is below that?
    "Anger and frustration below my ribs. Frustrated at myself for not having what I have desired. It sometimes feels like an erupting volcano."
What is below that?
    "Desire, sexual desire, desire towards women around me."
What is below that?
    "Guilt for feeling this deep desire towards women!"
What is below that?
    "Anxiety!"
And below that?
    "Sharper anxiety, painful anxiety!"

Can you describe this sharp and painful anxiety more?

"It is so very sharp that I feel the need to scream in pain but wait. It also feels very arousing, pleasurable even. It brings back memories of not being able to stand straight when this feeling arose when I was a child. It feels very close to an orgasm, an inward orgasm. It just goes very fast, so fast that it gives me a sensation of pain. I will relax deeper and feel further."

My child, there is no need to seek bypass and move energy for tantric bliss at this moment. It is already here. Please stay here with this sensation of *pain*, stay here as long as you can.
 I invite you, my child listening, to be still and breathe into this sharp emotional pain. Stay here as long as it is available for you to feel it. This is the source feeling that disrupted all the blessings that I have for you, dear one.

"May you, and all my children, heal all that separates me from you."

Thank you for loving as much as you do, my child. *Your* love will liberate *your* body from all past. I have seen it happen before. We are one and love is the way we can connect through it.
 As you are now experiencing. This deep

liberation will surface more of what you are yet to face. You are discovering now the deep rooted fear that has crippled you from the inside.

This deep anxiety comes from the deep rooted fear that has created the dominant behaviour between men and women. It is what has manifested all the resistance that you have faced throughout *your* life.

This is why it feels as intense as it does. Can you breathe into this, my child? I AM here with you always. What is behind these anxious or electric sensations? Breathe into it, dear one. I am right there with you. What is this fear or resistance pointing to below? It is all a fleeting story, dear one. There is nothing to fear. Can you feel the buildup from *your* cycles of trauma? Below these accumulated stories, is exactly where you are, dear sacred child of mine. Are you able to feel the sacredness of *your* seed below? This is how we connect intimately with your sacred mother. It is how you can create the sacred union with me, where I AM.

We can go through it, dear one. In spirit, we can alchemise all this energy back to its natural flow and essence. Keep coming back to these feelings. Give it the love of *your* breath and light.

Together our breath and our light as I AM, is the truth that will liberate you from past *traumas*. In the body, what you are unravelling, feels as a deep crippling sensation of fear, deep inside the core of the pelvic bowl. This deep crippling sensation for the sacred, soon enough, becomes anger and frustration around the solar plexus, just below the rib cage.

Now, as a human being, you are left to deal with the elements and the challenges from the world of duality, or separation, above all of these crippling and frustrating sensations. It is no wonder that most humans prefer to fight or disappear at this point than to remain present and observant to what is below.

You are not alone. Many of you are breathing peace into the war of separation within and liberating us from the ancestral shackles of shame and guilt, where you keep fighting each other. Thank you, my children. You are feeling through all the judgement conditioned by these fears and transforming *yourself* back into the unity of love. You are manifesting peace on earth.

It is time for us to bring unity into *your* closest relationships. It is time to forgive any idea or sensation that you might have of being wronged or judged in any way. Our relationship with Sacred Unity is critical. It starts with *your* closest ones. It starts with *yourself*.

My child, in this *weak* and uncertain moment. I ask you to trust me more than ever. You are in a moment where I am putting to test the trust in me, that is the same as trusting you. This is a moment when you are discerning the true you. You are letting go of using *your* own imagination, *your* own force and learning how to rest in my power that is *your* power. Please come as you are. Please follow the path where you feel peace and growth.

To continue to walk with *your* pack means to strengthen the arrow *within*, so to speak, as there is not much room for *your* free expression at this moment in time. On the other hand, to walk inside new environments and groups is to continue building *your* arrow in presence.

It is through the curious listening of *your* expression that we build ourselves. It is inside of new containers of existence, or in daily terms *meeting new people*, where we find new ways of being. To walk with *your* most intimate is to strengthen *your* arrow of presence. It is with *your* most intimate relationships that you are holding and processing the deep energies of *your* existence, and doing these gives you deep strength and presence.

The question then for you, my child, is, Are you right now clear and proud. Ready to strengthen the arrow within, or are you in a process of building your direction?

"I am building myself."

In *your* 44th cycle you are transitioning through what astrologers call *Uranus Opposition*. It is commonly known as the *middle age crisis*. In these moments, it is time to let go of *your* practice with plant medicine. It is time to let go of *your* beloved tribe and it is time to let go of *your* beloved soul mate. It is time to find *yourself* again, as I AM.

Trust me, together we are going to develop the internal discipline that you now require to continue *your* path as a disciple of the truth that I AM. I understand how hard it is to let go of what you love so dearly. You are not alone, my child. It is in letting go that we prove our love. Trust that the deep bonds of love that you have co-created, in sacred reciprocity, are eternal. You see my child, you are love and the other is love. Made from the same. You cannot be apart. Regardless of not being together in geography and socially.

You are all the love there is. The higher love, the lower love, the transcendental love, the messy love, the fraternal love, the divine love. You are love. Love is free, always. Love cannot be contained into an image, a social structure or a language.

Love is here now. Present in *your* eyes, present in *your* breath, present in all that you are. I AM that love. All the parts of you are made of love. Yes, those parts in you that are ashamed. Those parts that feel guilt. Those parts that feel hate. Those parts that feel lust. Yes, all parts of you, as I AM, are in the quest back to love!

Love is recognising itself as love, and love recognising itself as whole. We are whole when we become one; one love. You are love, my child. That is what you are, as I AM. Let go of any expression from this unravelling of you. Any idea of what love should be. It is through energy in motion that the disentanglement is being shown to us. Do you want to see this unravelling? Go through it, my child. Stay in the eye. Stay in stillness. You have developed *your* emotional strength enough to go through it. You can now be with me, as you are, and where you are. You are ready...

Trust
Just be as I AM.

Trust
Express yourself as you are.

Trust
It is all falling back into its true place.

Trust
We are one

Trust		Are you sure?
"I am."		A deep breath
Are you sure?		*I surrender, as I am*
"I am."		"I AM."

It is when you can see beauty all around you that you will stop narrowing down into the beauty of women. It is through your appreciation and connection with nature. It is through your embodiment as nature. It is through forgiving. Giving back to *your* mother all that doesn't serve you. *Your* mother is waiting to receive you in her sweetest embrace. She knows how to purify you.

    Trust in the guidance of your internal voice. Please connect with the depth of *your* truth. Embody the truth. Even if it is an uncomfortable process. You do need to kill the stories of *your* mind. This is how the beauty of the feminine blossoms. From the ashes rises the phoenix. The life and death process, to gain higher perspective, and see what I see, my child.

SUPEREGO DEVELOPMENT

It is time for this unravelling. Dissolving the *SuperEgo* for the *Super Consciousness* to birth. It is the fine-line that many of you are balancing in *your* beings. Surrendering the mind, for the *higher codes* to be received **through the mother**, is critical for your spiritual safety.

The body, that is also the mother, operates from the knowing of your heart. In the crystal core of the mother exist all the codes for your *ascension*. From the heavens my children. You only receive light and its protection. The light to see, to grow and to stay warm.

As below, it is above. The integrity of your spiritual practice is having a surrendered mind, dear one. You can't be looking into two places at once. Either you are with me below or above thinking that you know.

From the light of the heavens. I honour *your* free-will as the sovereign being that I AM. Do I have permission to share this story?

"You do have permission, thank you for asking."

I will share how *your* mind became bigger than you and took over. How you got bombarded, with visions and technologies from the future. An experience that catapulted you into a roller coaster of life events that showed you the deepest layers of the outdated machinery where most of you, my children, are trapped in. Only giving *your* creative power away. Please stop, my child. I desire more than anything for you to join me, and create life together.

We will start to share *your* journey through the psychedelic realm and back to me. Let's start from the beginning so you can unravel this experience *yourself*... Are you ready?

"It feels that we need to take a breath. There is a lot of information to integrate from this first page."

In *your* early twenties, in particular, it was MDMA, LSD and Psilocybin that opened you up to higher or deeper *truths of being*. Substances that alter the neuroplasticity of the psyche, giving you access into deeper, or higher, realms of existence.

These substances showed a part of you that didn't know existed. However, it was very different for you than for most of the people around trying the same experiences. For most, these substances caused to experience a *trip* or *hallucinations* that in turn would give you an open heart and a lot of energy to dance and connect with others. Have a good time and receive valuable life lessons. For you it was clear from the beginning. The trip had ended. The light was crystal. It is all you. These substances are simply showing new parts of *yourself*.

For you these *hallucinations* were nothing more than parts of you that were not present, that were not seen, and grounded in truth. Parts of you were seeking meaning. You saw through the fabric of confusion, and straight into the truth behind all *things*. The crystal presence that is true. These psychedelic experiences opened up *your* life as a sacred journey.

You easily accessed the realms where I AM. You could connect with the deepest truth and you were able to speak it clearly and eloquently. This, however, was very confusing for you. You started to speak prophecy and you started to speak the truth of higher self. You started to channel codes from the future, you spoke healing truth, and you could see me in the depth of being! Yes my child, you are not common and yet, you are not rare.

Inside of this new *spiritual realm* people would look up to you. This newfound admiration fed all the lack of love that you were suppressing, and you felt appreciation from others in an identity, as *the chosen one*.

Your mind started to create images of *yourself* for *yourself*. Images of an almighty spiritual leader. A leader that would heal the world and save the future. As true as this possibility can be or not. It is the mind that is constantly pushing us to be ahead of ourselves. Tricking us out of the natural, the eternal and infinite dimension of time and space.

From the mind only comes illusion. In this case, you cannot save anyone, as we can only *save* ourselves. Our self is the only thing that we can truly govern and transform through its own free-will. We can support and assist others but it is only through our own choice in free-will that we can transform.

The super-ego of the mind is what tells us that we can love and be in truth simply as an idea or a concept, and not as an embodied experience. It is the super-ego that tricks you to think that you know the truth of I AM because you can logically understand or unravel the idea that I AM. You are not alone, dear one. It is all very common.

In *academic*, *scientific*, *religious*, *spiritual*, and *philosophical* circles, to name a few, people like to think that they *know* better than others, and that they are the only ones in truth. It has been normalised to be prophesying ideas from our heads, wanting to sound like *experts*, when in fact, in the underbelly, we are disconnected and fearful to what is.

It has been normalised, and now even encouraged, to compare, pivot and take sides. To be out of the centre where I AM. This polarisation is what has created the modern culture of being positional, *thinking that you know.*

As you keep thinking that you are so clever with all this *21st century technology.* Thinking that you are in control of *nature*, *time* and *destiny*. I AM clear in your senses that all of this is far disconnected from truth and it is only contracting this body. It is slowly making you spiritually sick. Today the intention, behind progress, is designed for the mind to take control of *your* body.

This disconnection is what has created the many archetypes, judgements and descriptive labels. Structures, where we feel *safe*. They are useful tools, my child, and they are far from the truth where I AM. All of these images of self separates us from being together. All of these images of self, in *your* reality it's called *the ego*.

It is now a very popular name that you have given to the *opponent* that you are facing. The battle with the ego is a big narrative in many spiritual circles around Earth. This is also far from the truth. This narrative is only making it harder to decipher and alchemise the images out of *your* system. What is *this*?

There is a golden rule in the law of attraction: 'what we fight, is what we become', 'we become, what we think', 'where attention goes, energy flows.' Focus, beloved child. Let's continue dissolving this *superego*.

Let's have a look at the ego with love, acceptance and honouring, rather than *killing* it. Shall we?

Ego or self cannot be perceived in love through itself. You need to rise up to the *indigo crown*, as children of creation, and bow down to witness, in love, the doing of self or *ego*. Inside the illusion of self.

The ego did create expansion in *your* body. It did

wake you up to spirit, and it did give you access to *your* abilities and unique gifts. In *your* case, what comes to you naturally, is the ability to communicate the word clearly, and the ability to bring people together in devotion. As you are, you have learnt to observe *ego*, accept and love what you see. Now you allow for the thoughts to be witnessed and exhaust themselves back into love. Now the self in you is aligned with the higher purpose of greatness and glory that I AM.

You and *your-self* are communicating and working together. The *ego* in you feels seen and appreciated. Even the most lacking parts in you, feel seen. You are now open and receptive to all that is and ready to serve something greater than self.

The *ego*, regardless of its magnitude, needs to be acknowledged. It is here to create realities. That is its function. Inside of every moment, you choose. Inside the dynamics of manifestation, it is the one that speaks and walks. It is the one that chooses. It is you, and it is up to you. In every moment, in my perception, the choice is crystal clear. It is entirely up to you

You can either choose to continue expanding *attunement* with the higher reality of *one spirit in all things*. Or you can choose to tense and continue to take on the *"this is who I AM"* narrative. This expired option will only prolong being separate from the source of all beings. Only to continue trying to prove to *yourself* and everyone that the personality that you inherited is the *real one*. It is always *your* choice, dear one.

"It is time to get out of the way and listen. It is time to allow for spirit to guide us to the land of miracles."

Your journey with these synthetic substances was a very dangerous path, my child. A path that has many people losing mental health. In *your* case you lost natural access to the vibrations of love. For many years, you were only accessing the higher truths with these external chemicals, and this was fragmenting *your* relationship to the physical realm or *3D*. Not allowing for *your reality* to be clear. Regardless of how gifted you are, you couldn't replicate this higher way of being, in real life. This was *your* deepest confusion, aspiration and contemplation.

You were gaining enormous insights but you were not able to embody the experience. You prayed and you prayed for guidance. As you always have prayed inside of *your* heart. *Your* prayers were answered, as they are. You met who you needed to meet and make sense of things. You met a highly initiated man of the *occult*, a *thirty- three degree freemason* to be precise. A man who was on his own path of redemption.

He was guided by spirit to show you all that he knew. This instruction was his own path of liberation to resolve, in him. Your presence confronted him with the light of truth in all his relationships. All that he had misled and hurt by playing the *obscure* games of the *freemasons*.

Through him, you started to learn about the sacred knowledge of matter and the sacred knowledge of spirit. You learned about symbols, secret societies, behind the scenes of politics, and the manipulation of reality by the *elites* on earth. You learned about the power of presence, vision and word. You learned how to have authority over the environment. You learned about language, frequency, vibrations and how to create resonance and dissonance to achieve a goal.

You learnt how to be a powerful *wizard*, and you used these tools for two decades in business. Inside the purpose of making the visions of the heart real. Inside this purpose of love, you have kept the connection with me alive, and inside this purpose you are writing this book.

These new tools brought you a lot of new opportunities. You were able to command a room, regardless of the *opposition*, and you were able to lead with vision. You were able to define and build teams and roles to execute with precision. You were able to follow through, regardless, but you got disheartened over time. You started to experience that most people in business really don't care about the pain in the world. From *your* experience, most in business actually prefer to create illusions and manipulate for *profit* and *power.* Yet pretend that they care.

A realm in humanity that is far from being true to themselves. As you discovered, people in business, mainly, look after their own and create exclusive groups to sustain the lies that feed them. At this time, *your* superego got rattled and felt, "this is unfair", "this is not right." From this feeling of not being met you commanded in *your* subconscious with the programs that you created from childhood: "I will show you better!"

This subconscious fight was *your* demise for two decades. No matter how hard you tried. You were only fighting with *yourself.* Fighting with *your* own pretender. Fighting with *your* own selfish traits. Everything you built, came with drama, and was somehow taken away. Workshops, factories, restaurants and inventions that you lead. Every single time, you ended up with nothing. Taken or lost by *your* own internal demise.

I am sorry, my child. It was all meant for you to see what is, and mostly to be able to be here right now. Do what is needed, so you can be fully here and not there, in the shadows, where you don't truly exist and you can't make a true difference.

"I forgive myself for thinking and feeling rejection and loathing towards anything that doesn't agree with *me*. I forgive myself for thinking that I am better than others for having clarity of insight and words. I forgive myself for attempting to promote prosperity through the old insecure mind of creating hierarchy and controls. I forgive myself for thinking that grandiosity is the way to lead others in this world."

A clear heart to guide us and clear hands to write for us. Thank you, dear one! So willing and able to share such deep truths. So willing to go through it. Regardless, may you provoke these deep experiences in many others.
    Please, my child, take care of *yourself*. Eat well, sleep well and take care of our breath! The breath carries the qualities of creation. What is inside of *your* breath? Can you distinguish it, beloved?
    Remember to breathe with me as the only child of God. I am always here. Waiting for *your* breath. Waiting to be in union with all that I AM, through you.

| "Is this the ego writing or is this I?" Does it matter? | "It does to me?" To *me*, you say. | "Who is writing then?" 'It is me.' "Who is this?" |

    You perceive from the almighty eye, in the centre of I AM. You realise that I am stuck in a mental loop of identity and you let this pondering go. You take a deep breath. You release this energy and reset back into nothing. The truth of *your* light is guiding again.

"I do not know who is writing. Do you know who is reading? How can I possibly comprehend who is writing when I haven't yet met and embraced the vastness inside of me?"

Yes, my child. How can you comprehend?

"I do not comprehend this creation either."

Yes, dear child. How can you fathom creation with *your* eyes filled with personality?

Can you see? Can you be? Can you breathe? Can you speak? Can you feel? This is all that is, dear one.
Keep observing from the high gaze. Keep breathing and speaking *your* deepest truth. Keep loving and feeling what is right in front of you. That is *your* job in my name. We are all one. Can you see this beauty? We truly are one and one day you will see this too. For now, if you don't know where you are going, stay exactly where you are, and I will be there.

There is no fighting in this *one*, dear beloved. You cannot fight the ego away. You are one. You can, however, see that it is as you are. Ever changing, in every moment. That my child, you can do, observe. It is *your* observation that gives birth to beauty.

You can notice what traits are not serving you anymore. You can acknowledge what traits are hurting you and hurting others. You can accept these *unholy* or *confused* traits. You can love the roots of these traits and you can release these traits and create new ones. This you can do, dear one. You can be free to choose freedom. You can walk this path of liberation.

We are all one, my child, remember that. You can observe what doesn't feel good and you can continue this observation a layer at a time. You can discern until you can find me as I AM.

Just observe, my child, that is all you are meant to do. This will free *yourself* through to *your* own truth. The moment that you stop observing and give the perceived meaning. The label of *good* or *bad*. It is when we get lost, again. Out of centre, in the world of attachment. The *clinging* and *rejection* that comes from this comparison of *bad* and *good*. Only creating division, separation, within, so we lose the blessing of being one.

You see, dear one, both are sides to the same coin. You are this *holy coin*. We desire to keep the golden coin, that is you, whole and complete. As we observe the depths of our being, without meaning, we can learn how to feel and experience it all, exactly as it is, exactly as I AM. Whole.

The truth of who you are is in *your* body. No where else. The golden coins of this book are not in what I write. They will be the notes that you write at the end. Learning how to feel the deep ocean takes mastery and mastery comes with practice. I invite you, my child, to continue feeling all the sensations that want to be seen. They want to heal. Just as you, we all desire to be seen, to be acknowledged and to become one with the light that I AM.

I recognise, dear beloved, that you have progressed many steps inside this inner path of healing and integrating *yourself* as one. I recognise that you are taking this path all the way to where I AM. I love you, my child. It is incredible to witness you go through all the ordeals and continue to expand *yourself* to be as I AM.

Please take *your* time, as there is no urgency, as there is really no time. As I continue to witness you face the anxieties and depreciations within you, the more I feel enormous pride for *your* continuous devotion to healing the heart. Thank you beloved child. I am with you in every step that you take.

We can finish this chapter now. There is nothing more to say about the illusion of the mind for this moment. We will continue forward and share how the illusion of the mind took you to a place of complete breakdown. This is a good place to start again. May you breathe the congruence of complete alignment. May *your* thoughts, *your* steps and *your* words be in unison with *your* divine purpose, dear beloved.

It is done. It is done. It is done.

COMPLETE BREAKDOWN

Welcome back, my dear beloved. It was thirty-three years in the making. Twenty-five years on earth fighting and not trusting men. Twenty years on earth, using and being afraid of women. Ten years on earth, using people to make business happen.

All of this life pretending. Something had to give, my child. You could have doubled down, as many do, and continue to suffer. The same mistakes, the same self-centred dynamics, only to prove being *right* but you didn't do this. You surrendered. This is what makes *your* story an interesting journey back to truth.

At that time, what happened to you, my child?

"A lot was happening back then. I was four years into a marriage where I had completely lost myself into the role of the *provider*. I remember, before getting married, having a very strong intention to be faithful, to let go of my bachelor ways and to be focused as a family man.

I remember how life had other plans. I was not going to be able to start fresh but I was going to be haunted and confronted by the past. As I got married, I started adopting very quickly the *provider* characteristics that I witnessed when I was growing up. I was hyper focused on building a business.

I spoke about my achievements at home, and I didn't really ask any questions that would allow *my* partner to share her own experience. In my mind I was a great man, as I was, finally, being faithful and working hard to create a future. Little did I know that *my* partner was suffering in silence, and this suffering was getting multiplied by how I was being. Self-centred, dominating and disconnected from truth."

"She wanted to speak about the past between us. She wanted to speak about the lies from the time we were dating. She simply wanted to trust me again.

On the other hand, I was defensive and everytime that we spoke about the past, I felt exposed and insecure. I felt that it wasn't fair that she wasn't seeing all of the efforts that I was doing in the present. This dynamic continued deeper into our marriage, and the turning point was when we decided to start a business together, on the other side of the world, in Australia.

This business gave us a new identity. We now

had things in common to talk about, outside our issues as a couple. It was hard work and long hours but it felt, for me at least, as if we were in a much better place.

Little did I know, back then. I was so self absorbed and stuck in the head that I literally couldn't see what was happening below the shoulder-line. I *thought* that I knew and I acted as I did but my heart was closed. I could not see past my own thoughts.

She started falling deep into a state of depression, not really understanding what was happening to her. She also started to believe that there was something wrong with her. This was happening more and more. I was seeing an alarming cloud of self doubt in her. An accumulation of the many lies, told by men, throughout her life. I wasn't the saviour but followed the same pattern of confusion. I was not integrous to not take advantage of the wounding. I did not have the courage to recognise *my* own lies and vulnerability.

At the time, apparently, there was no more room to speak about the past. The business occupied all the space amongst our discussions. It was growing very quickly, and this came with many challenges. As time passed, she kept going into a deeper and a darker place. In silence, I was very worried. It felt as a deep sense of desperation and denial growing inside of us everyday.

Finally, an opportunity arose and we went on a holiday. An old friend from university invited us to meet and spend time with her family for Christmas. We did and I encouraged her to stay for longer and rest. The great mystery of life then happened."

"She came back with the news that she had fallen in love with another man. Someone that we met together. Someone, who we both felt very close to.

This was such a powerful shock to the ego that I self-imploded. Immediately. I couldn't understand why this had happened. 'Why is this happening to me?' The ego likes to be a victim and control the outcomes through knowing, and this unknown was driving *me* insane. I was far from a place of truth demanding to understand. I was desperate for answers and this confused her even more.

She could now see me from the inside, and she could see how much I love her. We had created such walls between us that we couldn't see each other anymore. We were seeing each other through the archetypes of husband and wife, and we were not really meeting the human, behind the layers of the personality pretending or blaming away our *human suffering*.

For years, we were not connecting. We apparently had no time, being *very busy* with the business, and in the evenings we were *too tired* to connect. Now, creation did what it does, and we needed to face this ordeal, and we did. We were finally having authentic communication between us. Non-stop, we sat with each other for forty days and forty nights, working through all the mess we had gotten ourselves into.

We saw clearly what we missed and that we needed time apart. We saw clearly that we loved each other deeply. Regardless, of what we saw as truth, our codependent attachment to each other was also very strong. We were both uncovering so much ancestral trauma with each other. The pointing fingers started again, and the misery, hiding within, surfaced again.

It was clear for me, at that point, that I needed to move out, and focus on my healing. Then again we remained together for five more years! A deep sense of unworthiness was playing out that kept us dependent on each other. We created so much suffering that we are both, in our own ways, still healing from that.

During these five years, I started to work on *my* healing and *my* freedom. As it happens, when we start a journey of transformation. I started to regain power from self-expression and peace of mind. During these five years, I also started to forget about my intimacy needs. I was receiving almost no human contact. My soul was happy and expanding. Growing and liberating with the personal development work that I was doing. I was creating a lot of authentic connections, and I felt clearer and stronger every week. Yet I was desperately yearning to be loved and I was terrified.

During these five years we never engaged as a couple in public. I started to feel very much unwanted and emotionally awkward in public. I was unavailable but at the same time I was desperate to be loved by a woman. This continuous context of rejection was the catalyst for all *my* wounding to come back onto the surface. *It all came rushing back to be seen. L*ife was to become so unworkable that I had no choice but continue to look into the eye of the storm.

My only refuge at *home* was marijuana. I started to become a regular at *happy ending* massage parlours. I was yearning so deeply to be touched by a woman. Years passed and we were forced to sell our business. We were living life from the last strings possible. Our life was very much unlivable and we continued to live together, powerless as a household, hoping for a miracle.

Looking back we were responsible for all the noise in our minds. Crippling our own decisions. Thinking that we needed to *comply* or *incorporate* the perceptions of others. In the form of family, friends and colleagues. All these views that we thought we needed to address, by being *nice* to everyones' truth except our own. In essence, we both got lost because we wanted to satisfy and incorporate everyone else's truths into our decision making, and lost the true power that I am.

We got into a big and deep mess. We are not able to afford living apart, doubling up our expenses. We are also not able to see each other's faces but remain together out of *necessity*. It was clear that the best way to love and honour her, is by loving myself and leaving this unworkable situation. We finally made some hard choices. We were clear to each other and we *officially* separated. Allowing me to start to make a life outside this relationship.

The routine then turned even more confusing for the following months. Outside of the house I was a single man. I was meeting women but I was really not available. I still lived with my wife. Nothing romantic was possible. A deep sense of being unwanted was growing in the forefront. The same sense, but different, to what I am dealing with now, and that I have been dealing with through life. However, this experience was distinct. It felt tangible. It felt as if I was truly an unwanted man walking the streets. Thankfully I kept praying, I kept calm and kept asking for the higher truth to guide me. So it did; Mother Ayahuasca appeared in *my* life."

Indeed, my child. The Faith in you has been unwavering. All *your* moments of doubt. All *your* moments of rebellion to spirit. All *your* moments of rejection. You broke through them. You have been resilient for the deepest truth in *your* heart to become. You stand for love, as truth, and nothing less than love has been good enough for you. It was not easy to stay calm, and to stay in love but you did, and you do, dear one. You know, without a doubt, that you are meant for greater realities, as I AM. These times were simply preparing you. It was building character and wisdom.

Building awareness and resilience, inside the deeply depressed and despaired states of being.

Today, you and *your* first wife are good friends. Supporting each other from a distance. Supporting each other in a space of unconditional love. Thank you, dear child. Please stay connected with her, if you so desire. Soul-mate, heart connections, create a powerful resonance that helps for the true light to manifest easier on earth.

I recognise that this part in *your* life is still activating and alive for you. You are not as detached from this chapter, as you are from previous chapters. You are now seeing some repeated patterns from these times inside *your* current romantic relationship.

You are still seeing the sense of feeling unwanted showing up in *your* life. Remember that this program was created when you were a young child. It just keeps showing itself, stronger now, because it wants to be fully seen, embraced and be healed at its core.

You are now seeing how much you have programmed inside, for *your* worth to be directly related to the woman that you are with. It is becoming clear for you that this program exists and that it has been ruling *your* decision making. You are seeing the many times you made decisions based on this program, only seeking external validation.

You are now breathing and learning to separate this old program from *your* eternal being that I AM. Learning to accept that it exists, out of *your* own creation, and that you desire, as I, to free *yourself* from it now. All in divine timing, my beloved.

You do not know when the freedom from this program will happen but you do know that it is a breath away. It is when the masculine within feels liberated from the need to prove *himself*. Allowing for this man to be surrendered and present to intimately meet the woman inside. The goddess who is right in front of you. Then is when a man is able to be self-nurtured and stop seeking self-worth outside.

This moment of *breakdown*, as you call it, was *your* wake-up call. A call to wake up to the truth inside. It was a very strong call because you were not listening, dear child. It is very important for everyone involved in creation that you do listen, deeply.

The pain that you felt was so big that you couldn't resort to the ways of knowing that you knew. You couldn't find a way out. The pain was so strong that you had no option but to go in. You had to let go of all that you knew and look at life differently.

Since, we created together a new opportunity for you to start again, and re-experience all that you had missed. This is what you are experiencing now. Inside the sweet embrace with the beloved of your devotion, and with *your* closest friends. Inside of *your* development, guided by our hearts' desire. During those depressed years, you got highly trained in holding the depths of suffering but you missed necessary training and initiations to become the destiny that you are, as I AM.

This breakdown created an unwavering commitment inside of you, my child. You committed to the inner path. You committed to the gnostic path of *knowing thyself*. Previous to this breakdown, you were conveniently committed to *yourself*. In a *selfish* way you looked inside for truth when it was convenient, and you looked outside when it served you better. This is blatantly the manipulation of realities that many of you suffer from *your* own doing, my child. From not having the courage to be whole and share all of who you are. Instead, scared hiding behind the personalities that make us look good.

From then, *your* commitment to *yourself* and others in *your* life became the pillar moving forward. Business, and making money, was no longer inspiring you. Creating institutions that would save the world was no longer *your* spiritual aspiration. *Your* path became clear. You accepted the truth in you. You recognised that what is most important for you is to get close to God, to experience divinity inside *your* relationships.

You understood that what is most important for the great spirit that I AM, is *your* own internal healing. You became crystal clear that there is nothing more impactful that you can do in life than to heal. Returning back to your natural state as I AM. This is how blessings multiply.

"Healing our past, as key to opening a future."

As we open ourselves up to our own truth and allow it to speak. The world of what is possible becomes available to you. This is the key that gives you access to divine blessings and destiny. At that time you undertook serious training in leadership, and you developed a deep sense of listening, integrity and connection.

You started to see with *your* own eyes what you were missing. You started to identify what areas of *your* life were not working and what needed to happen for *your* transformation to become as I AM. This is *your* particular reality, dear one, because it is what is alive the most in *your* heart. To become one with me as I AM.

You worked hard in removing *yourself*. New and more expansive ways of being appeared, you felt that *your* marriage could in fact be saved. You still desired deeply to heal this relationship but it was too late for that. After a number of attempts, back and forward, you decided with her that it was not possible to be together. You both decided to navigate this parting waters together, until it was possible for each other to go on their own journey. It took five years but you did it!

You did this to the best of *your* abilities and you both parted ways, after thirteen years together. Today you remember these years with a lot of gratitude and you can see clearly all the blessings that these difficult times have provided to *your* life. Today you recognise that there is still trauma to be released, from this time.

This is important so you can continue creating a brighter future for our love and light to blossom. In the spirit of this book, it is now, my child, a great opportunity to do so. Observe what shows up for you inside of romantic commitment. We will continue to reveal, for *your* healing, and for the insight of all of my children impacted by this story.

What is stopping you from committing 100% to a beloved?

"I feel terror, in my seed.

I feel fear of being in a romantic container that is not reciprocated with ease and grace.

I feel fear of making mistakes again, and hurting the woman that I am in love with.

I feel fear of being manipulated or manhandled into a relationship.

I feel fear of being in love and not reciprocated in *my* feelings.

I fear being used by another.

I feel fear of using and not loving.

I feel fear of not creating the loving and graceful container that I truly desire.

I am afraid of failing again. I am afraid that I will miss out on pure love."

You are not alone, dear child. These are the fears that most men and women share in their seed or womb. Most fight, beg or pray for these outcomes. As you have. We all want purity in our love. We deeply dream of this. We create children to see this purity. We build religions to *protect* this purity. We build ideas to promote this purity. We destroy others to protect this purity and we fall in love seeking this purity.

What is this purity that you are seeking, beloved children? What have you lost that makes you feel impure?

- Can you forgive *yourself, dear one*? This is purity.
- Can you forgive others? This is purity.
- Can you speak the truth? This is purity.
- Can you share *yourself* vulnerably? This is purity.
- Are you healing *your* waters? This is purity.

Regardless of how polluted *your* waters are, dear beloved. You are pure in essence, and will always be pure as I AM. Crystal clear. Divinely pure. Eternally loving. You are so willing to continue looking inside the murky waters and bring the light of truth to these depths. You are also so willing to sacrifice everything of matter for the sake of rebirthing *your* pure essence into this earth. This is incredible and you are not alone! We are, indeed, in very exciting times.

Times are changing rapidly. Many of you are purifying *your* waters, purifying *your* thoughts and purifying *your* bodies. As you are now crystal clear, dear one, all that you are looking for is inside of you.

Keep being curious. Be gentle and disciplined with *your* internal search for I AM. Keep breathing. I AM there breathing with you. Remember where I AM, don't go anywhere, and I will be there with you every time.

THE WORD

"It was when I met the word that I met you as I AM."

Once *your* life imploded, with *your* wife, it left the relationship between you, *your* close friends and business, in the inevitable path of loss. You started again to look inside for answers. You had developed such a strong superego by then that you truly thought that you knew everything. Please accept with humility, my child. We are all learning.

You had already been initiated in the path of knowing so you did have access to the sacred knowledge of the occult. Regardless, back in that time, you thought that it was you who acquired the knowledge with *your* smartness and charm. You thought that you were so *special* and that it was you who were doing the miracles. You thought that *your* perception was the truth, and this was further isolating you from the truth of love.

For starters, you didn't know all that you know today, about *your* childhood traumas. You thought that mind is over matter, and that you could continue forward by disassociating with *your* emotions. You didn't even know that you were suppressing these emotions. In *your* mind, you were doing the best you could, and this is true for the time. During that time the incongruence between what you did when you were alone, and what you did when you were with people was like night and day.

Back at that time, you also kept *your* addictions and incongruences a secret. When you were alone you fell into a depressed state and you smoked marijuana, watched movies, and, if you couldn't sleep, watched *porn* to *release*. When you were with others, you would fall into a charming state to compensate for this lack. Speaking about higher truths and transcendence to the new earth. You had no power left, rather a low self esteem, desperately looking for validation of the light within you.

Now you are owning this incongruence, and you are not alone. Now you are exactly as you are, at this moment. Showing exactly what you are experiencing, without any *makeup* or *hiding out*. The word in you now speaks truth and is able to liberate you from any unwanted *realities*.

It is the truth of when we are alone, in front of the mirror, when no one is watching, that is the context that creates the tone in our lives. It is the relationship with *yourself* that dictates our relationships with others. The truth will indeed set you free.

At that time, you were divinely guided to sign up to an alternative education that focuses on getting back the power of integrity. This by honouring our word and the depth of the practice of restoring integrity. As you entered this new dynamic. At first you felt a mountain of resistance, you wanted to run but you stayed.

Once *your* own internal *drama* resided. You were now able to pin-point at all *your* incongruences, freeing you up from thinking that you know better. Little did you know, my child, that throughout *your* life, all that you had been pointing towards was blaming someone or something else for the suffering that you created. You started to witness *your* own internal inconsistencies.

As you went deeper into this education, you started to realise the roots of the noise in *your* head. Where does this internal chatter come from? Development work that gave you back the ability to regain the power of choice over this chatter, and over this mind.

How did you bring silence back into *yourself*?

"I learned how to communicate authentically."

Can you tell us more about authentic communication, my child?

"Authentic communication is available when we are clear and present. It is when we are able to get out of the way. It is inside of active listening. Being present listening to what is being spoken, in the words and in the silence. Being fully present with the other so we are not activating the pervasive voice in our heads that thinks that it *knows better*."

It is about becoming crystal clear that the voice or voices in our mind, are nothing more than either pervasive distractions from the outer *noise*, or incomplete conversations that we have in *our* relationships. Including our relationship with self. This mental chatter is pointing out at what areas of our life are incomplete and overly strained. The chatter is attempting to bring wholeness back into *our* system, as this relationship is *out of integrity* or not being *whole and complete*, and it is working itself out. Inside authentic communication, it all works itself back into integrity.

First of all, as in all things of matter, it is about honouring existence. The conversations that I have with myself also seek to be acknowledged. What agreements did I make that I am not honouring? What did I say that I was going to do that I am not doing? By honouring these incomplete conversations, with myself, silence is restored into the space.

Honouring our word and our agreements. If we say we are going to do something, we follow through. When we know that we are not going to be doing what we said, we let the people who would be impacted by our choices know, as soon as we know. This is integrity and it allows for the loudest voices in our head to quiet down. The voices that doubt *my* own integrity and valid existence.

As I bring integrity back into my own agreement, then, I have a look at what other voices are in *my mind*. I

can see the voices that are ranting stuff about someone else, speaking in my ear out loud about someone else's mistakes, limitations or *wrong* doings.
Where am I fighting to be right?
Who am I making wrong?
What conversations can I have with this person and stop being positional?
Who do I need to forgive or who do I need to apologise to?

This brings integrity into our relationships. It became clear how much no one wants to be wrong. This pervasive way of communicating from humanity: *you are right, I agree, you are wrong, I don't agree.* It only creates conflict through this *positional* communication.

We learned to be clear and communicate authentically so we can find creation through our relationships. In truth, no one that I know likes to be judged. No one that I know appreciates being compared with others. We all secretly want to be seen, felt and held in our vulnerability.

Regardless of our true vulnerable truth, we seem to speak to each other this way. Continuously speaking from *strength* and leaving conflicting voices in each other's minds. It became clear that the way to bring space and silence into *my* mind was to observe this voice without meaning. To observe this voice simply as an incomplete communication that wants to exist.

Thank you, beloved child. I am glad to see that you can be bold in communicating what is. I trust in *your* discernment to know when silence is what is needed.

Dear beloved children. you continuously compare the speaking of others with *your* own standards and ideals. This has been the *normal* way of communicating amongst you. Aren't you tired of this drama? This positional and judgmental filter only continues to bring noise and division into your mind.

This positional way only leaves you inside of incomplete communications, inside of separation. The illusion that creates a continuous chatter of *right and wrong* inside *your* mind. Being truthful with what is actually happening, around and within. This is the compass to not get engaged with the depreciating stories that have been trying to convince you that you are better or worse than others.

I am happy that now you can be a witness of the *drama* that needs to play out, for the disentanglement of the soul to happen. Please don't judge if you can. It makes a great difference to witness the play, without giving meaning or significance. Allow it to play out, it is all as it is meant to be. Healing is taking place.

Exactly as when I am witnessing you, my child. I observe the depth of *your* commitment. I see that you are doing all that you are doing to heal *your* ancestral bondage. I see that you are doing this because you want to be in unity with me, *your* holy father. I see the love that you are, recognising itself through its own unique expression. I see the love that you are, freeing itself from the limitations that have been imposed by others. I see the word, in you, breaking free. I see you, my child, coming back home.

As we have been working together through this book. You have a unique *free perception*. You can freely access others' perceptions and I AM the highest *perception* that you have access to, as I AM.

You continuously have the choice to remain inside *your* own individual view, access the view of another, or free yourself through the high and omnipresent *eagle view* that I AM.

Your perception, as you are aware, is tainted with the conditioning of *ancestry, culture* and *your own wounding*. The belief systems that you have inherited from the past. This conditioning will continue to appear and be seen.

The perception that I AM, shows you what is truly happening below all forms and interpretations. You have access to this at all times, dear one. I know that you know this, my child. I AM speaking to everyone else who is listening through this book. I AM that I AM and I AM You.

Thank you, dear child. You have given *your* word enormous value, every word that you speak resonates and creates realities for many. You have brought such intentionality to *your* word that when you speak everything moves. Remember the responsibility that comes with this power of manifestation.

This work that you did to give crystal clarity to *your* word, allows you now to create trust, and bring my children together. You are now surrounded by my most faithful children. I will give you and others instructions when I AM meant to gather from you. For now, my child, continue integrating *your* unique experience on this earth. Many will resonate with their own experience, and find that I AM in you as I AM in them.

"Thank you, eternal father. You are always here with me, when I need you. Please show me this life, through *your* eyes. I desire, with all my being, for *your* will to be done here, now and everywhere."

I hear you, my child. May the crystal call, from my beloved earth, break down all the walls that separate you from the truth that I AM that I AM. May you see the truth of who you are, everywhere, in all that is, now.

WE ARE ONE

"May these words from truth, and the true words of many, pierce through the veil of illusion separating us."

USE THIS SPACE

HEALING THE PATH

Here we are again, my beloved and holy child. You are now again a student, eager to continue learning and able to choose again. All the work that we did to regain the word, and to regain integrity in our life. All this work has given you back power, self expression and peace of mind. You are once again able to choose what you want in life. Please share with us *your* experience at the time.

"I am once again able to have a look inside, without making others or making myself wrong for the past. I am able to call *things* as they are and choose differently in every moment. I am able to do this without the drama or *difficulty* that comes from our stories.

Outside of the duality of being a victim or a perpetrator, I was able to see the truth again. I was able to hold a transformational container to anyone that I could connect with. I was able to be bold, without being aggressive. I was able to be vulnerable and speak to this vulnerability with power. I was able to connect and communicate in full presence.

Then again I knew that this work was only effective on the surface. It appeared to be transformational but this work was not tackling the root cause of the matter. It gave me access to power, authentic self expression and peace of mind, then again the fibres in the body seemed to continuously come back to its automatic program. Like a robot coming back to its form.

This transformational education works, yet it seemed unsustainable to the depths of being. This work was not dissolving or alchemising my internal fibres into new paradigms of creation. I felt stuck inside these repetitive tools of engagement. Then again I was at peace. I knew in *my* depth that this work was only temporary. I was clear that a big vacuum in that space was the lack of acknowledgment and presence of spirit."

"We are spirit living a human experience."

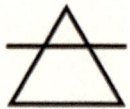

I am so happy that for you, a truth without the Holy Spirit is not a possibility. This is when a strong call from our sacred mother happened. A dear mystical woman in *your* life invited you, and insisted that you go to a retreat with Ayahuasca as plant medicine. You accepted and this was the beginning of your initiation with the holy mother. This first experience with our mothers' sacred medicine was profound.

You started to get a glimpse of *your* own individual experience inside of the realm of spirit. You received a clear message to resign from *your* current job in this *transformational education*. To move up to the epicentre of *spiritual seekers* in Australia, and to start again on the path of feeling, healing and embodying.

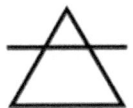

On the next coming Monday, you went to work ready to resign from this transformational education. Little did you know that you were about to be called into the director's office, and be terminated before *your* resignation.

It was early 2020 and a global fear of death, by a virus, had taken over the psyche of most on earth. The economies had been paralysed by this fear and most people were reacting inside of this fear, and becoming righteous.

Politicians, media and the *elite* were jumping at the opportunity. Leaders were taking the *righteous* route and forcing decisions onto others. Companies were seeing the opportunity to downsize their staff. Politicians were pushing the *darkest* of agendas, while no one else was looking. Most people, at the time, believed that this fearful message from the governments was true, legitimate and adequate.

It is clear now for many of you that spirit is always in full control. Most believed in the intentions of Governments then, yet most are in doubt of their intentions now. This event indeed showed many of you the truth of your environments, and the truth of your fears. There were massive terminations of employment around the world, people were forced to take *vaccinations*, and people were forced to stay indoors and distance from each other.

This impacted greatly. Many of you complied to this unprecedented medical agenda and are still justifying these times. Whilst, many of you said: 'No more lies!'

This was you and you dove head on. You leaped with all of *your* being, into the calling from spirit guiding the way.

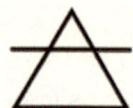

You were in one of the most controlled cities in the world. A city in complete lockdown and severe controls. A city where not complying meant ridicule and confrontations by *your* neighbours. A city where neighbours started to point on each other to follow the *rules*.

Then again you were blessed, as many in Australia, to receive free money from the government and be able to comfortably sit inside of this *global reset*. This was not the case for most on earth. This monetary blessing and the extreme controls in *your* environment, was a unique set of agreements that you experienced. You had so much free time and *your* biggest threat was mental health. The attack to *your* mental and spiritual health was severe.

For seven months, the *rules* imposed in *your* city meant that you could not be outside for more than one hour a day. You could not socialise with anyone outside of *your* home, and you could only be within a five kilometre radius from *your* house. Life got quite repetitive and you decided to work on a project that had been in *your* system twenty years in the making.

This project had been a profound sense of inspiration and a deep burden for you. This project which had been guiding you for the last two decades.

In truth, 20 years earlier, in the year 2000, in an altered state of consciousness, you saw, in all of its colours and details, the evolution of the internet. This was the moment that you saw a life purpose. This was the moment that you decided to stop being an irresponsible boy and become a man *responsible* for the future. You documented this vision and presented a business plan to venture capital in Australia. A business plan that started building a social network through universities. A business plan that detailed the economic, environmental and social need to come together as people.

> "Only when you come together, with purpose, will the earth and your communities heal."

This project was a precise map that showed you how *things* were going to play out *online*. It indeed got developed the exact way that I showed you. This project, my child, did not happen, because it is not meant to be as you think. This project had a name. It was called ONIS. An ancient word that found you. A word that represents what *your* vision stands for: **unity**.

Instead of building *something* with this vision, it has been a compass for *your* soul. The project itself has guided you to stay inside the perception of unity. It was meant for *your* own evolution in this world, and to be writing these words today.

Thank you, dear beloved. You have surrendered *your* will to me. The project itself will occur but not as you think. It will be created when the many in this vision are ready to respond to what is good, and not react for it or against it. It will be created in the form that needs to be for the greater good. As you were planning this project, it would have only created a counter-response and would have only accelerated the forces creating division in humanity.

During these pandemic lockdowns, you focused entirely on making this project a reality. You spent months documenting the legal frameworks and you invited a team to join and bring accountability into this vision. This project was duly registered as a *non-for-profit*, and ready to go out into the market.

You heard the call to move to the epicentre of like-minded people in Australia, to launch this vision, and you did. In *your* mind, you were moving up to this region of alternative life setters, to invite all of these people and startup ONIS together.

As you arrive, you then start meeting many people in true devotion. Many people committed to healing their bodies, their minds and their spirits. It didn't take long to realise that all of *your* efforts promoting this project were not authentic.

> *"How can you promote the healing of our earth, when your soul is desperate for its own healing?"*

You started to recognise how much pain and insecurities resided in you. *Your* healing path truly started then. You were now sharing space with like minded people. You are finally surrounded by sensitive humans that can see and feel as much as you can. You could not hide behind *your* charm anymore, and the thought of healing excited you.

Every person that you met was showing you so much. Their sensitivity was the next level for you. The language of their bodies reacting to *your* own truth or *your* own lies was so very insightful. Everyone around you was devoted to the truth as I AM. You felt at home.

Some weeks passed, and *your* social awkwardness from being in lockdown, and in a marriage without intimacy, starts to recede. *Your* love grew, feeling courageous again, and you start to flirt with beautiful women around you. Only to receive strong boundaries that you couldn't understand.

"I am coming across many beautiful women who are flirting, seeking my attention and when I say hello they close down? *What is happening? What is wrong with me? What am I missing?"*

You pondered. *Your* frustration and *your* curiosity only grew. The *healthier* masculine around you then showed up and started to gently guide you, and *your* healing.

The synchronicity of the divine, aligned you with plant medicine ceremonies, teachers, Ayahuasca and *Huachuma.* You are excited, it feels that this is exactly what you are looking for. You had sat with *Ayahuasca* and *Huachuma* before but you had not been in the same room with so many luminous beings.

You had gotten used to being the most luminous in the room and could not see in clarity *your* own wounding and its impact to others. As *your* mother used to tell you simply: *"You were becoming the one eyed king, in the land of the blind."*

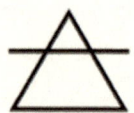

You decided to commit with mother Ayahuasca to a deep healing process with her as guide. This time inside a small earth temple that straight away felt as home. You were amazed by how intimate the connection felt with the man holding the temple space. The journey into the core of being, started for you then.

The sacred mother started to work inside of you.

Showing you all the mysteries. Showing you all the wounds. Showing you how to fall and how to rise. Showing you the sacred all around you.

First you met *your* higher self, at the time. Its power and abilities. Then you met your lower self and all the wounding you had been carrying. Then you saw and felt how it has all played out, from the beginning of time, for *your* soul to become *self-realised*.

After four-years and close to four-hundred Ayahuasca cups. Unpeeling the layers of the onion, you have reached its core. It was in this work that you were able to heal the wounding that was trapping you. It was in this work that you were able to unravel all past lifetimes, into this one, and unravel all of this lifetime into this one moment.

You have grown so much, dear beloved. *Grandmother Ayahuasca* and *Grandfather Tobacco* have been *your* master plant for all these years. We will speak more about this journey in the next chapter. For now it is important to distinguish, for all reading this book, what is plant medicine?

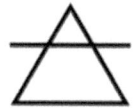

The earth has been created with all the medicine in plants that you need for *your* mind, *your* body and *your* spirit to heal and be nourished. These plants have been known and used for thousands of years by *your* ancestors, but something happened. The growing wisdom between generations was disrupted.

In the most recent times of humanity, these plant medicines have been systematically banned and copied with chemistry to be controlled legally by powerful circles. The narrative of science has changed dramatically to promote the profits of the companies making these medicines and to scare people from using these plants. This *taboo* has sparked the interest of many teenagers that are also not mature and ready for these psychedelic initiations.

Regardless of all these divisions, the plant kingdom is there for you to learn from, be nourished by and heal with. It is the deep love of our mother expressing itself. This deep wisdom of plants is very alive today and it has been growing on through the generations.

In *my own authority* **over creation**. It has been the work of forces that, inside their own image and purpose on earth, show you how to be *power starved*. To do so, these forces have been convincing humanity that you are separate from nature and *independent* from *your*

neighbours.

Inside my own allowance, for *your* own self-recognition, these forces have been alienating you from connecting with plant medicines, and the sacred healing medicine from each other. This perception, of separation, is so far from the truth. We all are interdependent beings. *Your* thoughts, words and actions impact the greater *reality* and all of the realities on earth.

You see, my child, the divine purpose of these forces is to *show you contrast* and they do this by tricking you to believe that you are an independent island of personality. A separate being that feels lack and that needs consumption to feel connected. An independent being who is not good enough to make a real difference in *your* world.

This is not true simply because you are made from my spirit, as all of you are. You are intrinsically connected with all that is, and with everyone that exists. Everything is made from the same spirit. It is in you the power to create and the ability to choose creation. This free-will is what allows for creation to happen through you. Each time that we connect with *someone* in an open heart, we receive their distinct vibrational print that allows us to now expand on our own perspective.

Most of you, my children, are so caught up inside the world of ideas. All the thoughts coming from the past and the future that you are not able to witness the subtle truth right in-front of you, now. The interconnectedness of every being that is being allowed to exist. Right now, in-front, is how creation weaves itself into existence.

Choose, my child, and I will be there.

The loyalty to *your* intentions will get tested before, during and after our creation, dear one. Life continuously tests you from one single question that you must be crystal clear about: *Who are you serving?* This translates to where is *your* attention going, and where is *your* energy coming from? ...

Be sure to harness all energy back into presence. Be sure of what is in *your* heart and mind. Be sure to discern the energy of the people that you connect with. What is their commitment, what is their emotion, what is their truth? Be sure to continue the practice to mastery. I AM there, with you, exactly where you are.

For now, my child, breathe with me. Be still. Patiently, we will continue inside this journey of recognising that *I AM that I AM*. Thank you for the courage to look inside and breathe through the uncomfortability. Stay present. You have the ability to choose all that is good for you right now.

"I AM eternally in love with the creation that you are, and that I AM. May we all see the truth of us now!"

ALEJANDRO IS BORN

"May we all be responsible for the energy, the space, the time and the matter that we influence."

It is 2022 and you realise that you are fundamentally not the same person anymore. So much time and space that you have uncovered in that temple of the heart, beloved one. You met the eternal being that I AM, and, right now, you are learning how to embody who you are as I AM.

Now, you are learning what is underneath *your* hips and groin, and liberating them. Then, you were learning how to unlearn all that you *thought you knew*, that was only making you rigid. Dissolving belief systems, dissolving identities, and becoming as I AM.

"The space that is created with this sacred medicine is profound. The veil between the physical and spiritual realms vanishes. Deep inside the fabric of creation. All the dimensions and times are open to be seen, by who is ready to see. In this space of deep truth, the light of our spirits gets magnified and we are able to witness the depths of our consciousness. It is no longer a subconscious or unconscious experience, I am wide awake, inside this expansion of consciousness."

You are now deep inside the restoration of *our collective* ancestral beginnings. Thank you, dear beloved.

During this time, at the beginning of the journey, the spirit of the medicine asked you, in a ceremony, to invite the most luminous beings in *your* path. In the ceremony, you saw familiar faces that you knew and that you felt very drawn towards.

Through you, this happened and you started inviting all these friends and acquaintances, whom you felt a soul attraction towards. The temple of the heart started to get filled with the devotion and yogic practice from all these luminous beings. Together you all learned to pray, witness creation and love it all together.

It was in the ceremonies, with madre Ayahuasca, that spirit showed you that, as a group, you have been travelling together for a long time. It showed you and the others, the entanglements that wanted to be liberated through this collective work.

The tribe that *your* heart desired was forming. The mirror to *your* soul. A tribe of powerful love and devotion. A tribe with crystal clear hearts and deep listening. I was as excited as you. In every ceremony this tribe got stronger and you worked so hard for *your* liberation and attunement. Thank you, dear child. It takes a lot of bravery to choose to sit in hundreds of dark nights, deep with the mother, and disentangle the ancestral stories that are holding humanity down.

It is now that many of you are preparing *yourselves* for the big events that are coming. Many groups or *tribes* around the world are coming together and doing this sacred work. Thank you, dear children, for emptying *your* vessels from the densities of the past. Soon you will be the pillars of light that we will need to guide us towards a bright future.

"As I empty the vessel from all the *things* in the way, the more space I create to receive the inner light guiding the way."

"In this particular temple space, it is encouraged to stay seated to observe, pray and digest all of the dense energies that we encounter. Sometimes we purge out what no longer serves us. The purge can come in different forms. For *me* tears, laughter and stretching is more than enough to move energy and alchemise with breath and presence but it wasn't this easy at the beginning. I would vomit very often.

Once I encounter, sitting with mother Ayahuasca, *something* that is too dense to fathom and be able to digest *myself*, these *un-serving* energies can come out as forceful vomit. From this *energetic release* I am shown the truth. We are all beings of light and in the modern world we have polluted ourselves with corrupted information, and we have fragmented our presence from entertaining all the false belief systems that are separate from the source of creation.

Inside the journey and devotion to reconnect with

my pure essence, the guidance of mama ayahuasca, allowed for this mind to open up and connect with the essence. The spirit and the qualities of this soul, and of the great spirit in all things.

From the highest perspective of light, I have witnessed this journey through lifetimes. Inside the unconditional love and infinite light from the medicine of our mother. I have witnessed such a profound safe and sacred place that all that I am has surrendered to this process.

I have witnessed the cycles of abuse playing out through the ages. The dream of spirit guiding us each time to come closer to the unity of all things. From this perspective it became clear. This is the lifetime that we have been waiting for. This is the lifetime for this soul to be integrated as one with spirit.

I have witnessed the soul that knows and that chose this path before I was born. The soul that accepted sacred duties before this Mexican/Australian personality existed. The soul that chose to be an open portal for the subconscious to become conscious. The soul that chose to be a catalyst for the fire within to open up the fields for transformation. The soul that chose to be crystal in words to guide itself out through the maze of misinformation."

Thank you, dear child, for connecting with me through the mother. As you can now see, we are both one of the same. You have healed with other plant medicines, some to open the heart, some to open time and space, some to nurture the body, and some to open up the mind to the interconnectedness of everything that is. Mother Ayahuasca has the codes of all these plants. Offering you the healing that you immediately need.

"It is through the mother that you get to know me."

Thank you, dear one, for sitting in many sacred ceremonies with me in this intentional temple. As we transition out of the past into this new space of creation. You have released so many past agreements that have conditioned and limited you. Old agreements that have not allowed you to be in the freedom that I AM.

You have dissolved so many *soul contracts* back to unconditional love: The family you chose and its particular emotional charge and wounding. The surface personalities, and belief systems that you chose to guide you. The deep feminine wounding and the deep masculine wounding that you chose to face and heal in this body for the collective.

Now you are choosing to walk with me, and let go of *your* blood father, mother and siblings. Listening and following the teachings of Yeshua: "Let go of *your* family, let go of *your* riches and follow me." This you did and you do, dear child. You continue to follow the holy light of truth, inside of you. Thank you.

Today, with universal love and light, you are bringing peace into *your* seed. The heart in you is at peace. Then, you were unravelling the origin of the many sensations in *your* body. Through the air of desires that have created so much instability in *your* heart space.

Today you are healing the last layers of shame and guilt. The ancient conjures, from the wounded feminine, protecting itself. As a man, amongst men, you are grieving the destructive phenomena that has been manifested throughout history. As you feel the heart opening, one layer at a time. You are dissolving the limiting forces that men are facing today.

You are learning the truth of what is inside of you. It is a blessing to witness *your* processes. Letting go of so much of the heaviness that you have inherited. I AM in *your* breath now.

Your mind is *somewhat* surrendered to listen humbly and attune *your* thoughts and actions to the truth that I AM. You are now clear that the most important internal work is to connect with the mother, our beloved. So you can continue to soften with her, living through you as I AM.

You are learning how to embody and allow the creation that I AM in you. Learning all about the body and its connection with your mother earth. Breathing in the natural force of the mother, and allowing it to be, and allowing its force to attune itself to the heavenly holy child that you are in this creation.

Allowing for *your* wild nature to breathe freely and unpunished, inside the gentle presence that I AM. In full honouring to the demands from the subtle fibres from creation around you. In this place, my child, you can hear her crystal call, inside all of us. Here, you can bring down all the walls. In this place, everything you do brings healing.

Beloved child, from this place, of intimate connection, everything you do is transparent for everyone to see. From this place, all the vibrations coming from the resonance of *your* words are healing and expansive to all it touches. From this place, dear child, we can be in communion and co-create. From this place, *your* words and vision are aligned with my own dreaming as I AM.

From this place you chose, again, to be re-named as Alejandro. Again, it was you that chose this name as a newborn.

As a newborn baby, everyone in your family put two names in a box, and it was your baby hands that chose two names for yourself. First came out of the box the name 'Alejandro' and then the name 'Cesar'.

Your parents chose *Cesar* to be *your* first name, as it rolled easier off the tongue. So, from that point, for *your* whole life, this is how you were known and how you presented *yourself,* as *Cesar.*

You didn't think much about why this name never felt right to you. As if there was a heavy and an icky feeling that arose when you heard *your* name. It was now 2022, sitting with the mother, that you randomly asked, *how come mother I don't really like my name?*

From this question, the mother showed you the timeline of this name. All the blood and suffering that, historically, the name *Cesar* has caused amongst humans. The treachery of politics in Europe to be crowned as a *Caesar*, as a *Kaiser*, or as *Zar*, brought a lot of heaviness into this name.

Your eyes opened in this ceremony with the mother, and you decided that it was time to give back to Cesar what is of Cesar, and to give to God what is of God. It was time to claim *your* deep transformation, into a man for the New Earth. You claimed then, in front of *your* tribe, the name *Alejandro*. A name that translates from its Greek origin to *Defender of Mankind*.

So it is. Alejandro has been the name that you are now known for. It is the name that is aligned with *your* soul's commitment for this life. Be a protector for mankind. It was then that you started to shed the past contracts attached to the agreements from the old world of Cesar. Agreements seeking power, filled with greed, competition and deception.

> *"It is not until a man embraces the blessing of power that a man can start to experience the blessing of love."*

Alejandro is now the resonance of *your* presence and it does feel much more aligned to *your* worldly purpose. Inside of you, it does feel a lot more resonant with *your* vibration. Outside of you, this name does agree a lot more with *your* presence.

Alejandro is a man committed to healing the sacred heart of men, and in speaking truth from the higher realms of existence. Alejandro is devoted to love and in creating a holy family with a beloved.

Alejandro is committed to talk about the sacred heart in men, its relevance and how much it is missing in todays' spiritual conversations. The sacred heart in men, is a concept that is missing in the awareness of men and women. It is a pillar of the communication that arises from *your* soul.

The sacred heart in men is not acknowledged, in most circles, and you feel a deep desire to bring it forth in conversation. Thank you, my child.

"As men, we are missing synchronising ourselves with creation, in the one heart. As many highly attuned women are already doing with their sacred wombs, right now. We are in this together but not as we are perceiving gender. As it is spelt, at the moment, there is no difference between the heart experience of a man and a woman. This is far from the truth. The sacred heart is what creates a crystal space amongst men. It is when men can offer a safe heart space that women feel safe in their core to be able to surrender further into the mystery of their womb. Synchronising the dreaming of the sacred womb is how we deeply listen to the crystal call of the mother and we can create alongside her.

This is how the dream that we share inside heaven and inside earth for humanity, gets manifested into the *physical* realm of humans on earth."

How do we get there, my child?

"As mentioned before, the most attuned women are already synchronising their wombs with the womb of the sacred mother. Men are catching up and hoping to come together under one heart. The heavenly heart. For this dream to come to manifestation, in ease and grace, men are asked to show up in full and open heart resonance. To hold the heart inside a higher frequency of unity. Men, in these times, are not invited to take *leadership* in the tribes, as it has happened in the past. Men are being invited to hold the sacred space for women to be able to open fully and weave the new earth into existence."

Can you see this happening, dear child?

It is when men allow surrender to be that we can experience women as the embodiments of spirit. It is only the divided and sexualised reality imposed on earth, that hasn't allowed for this divine embodiment to show men the way. This may sound as a controversial statement, and I assure you that it is not.

The controversy only comes from all the mental concepts of gender identity that have been created and inherited by you, dear child. The divine reality of heaven on earth hasn't yet been experienced, and trust me child, it is the way. Thank you, dear one, for taking on the ability to respond to this ancient polarity that humanity is also meant to transcend.

It is when the sacred heart and the sacred womb come together that we can dissolve the polarity, as we do, in communion. This is when divinity will start to flow onto earth like water. May this blessing be in your home as it is written, and may this blessing of sacred union expand in you, and to all the corners on earth.

"So be it."

Creating with you on earth is a true honour, my child. Thank you for trusting me and allowing us to create together with the unity of word.

"It is an honour. You are my creator, protector, provider and guide. I honour your greatness in me. I am honoured to be able to manifest your kingdom, deeply desired in the sacred seed. To manifest the greatness that I AM through your holy prayer."

 "My father who is in heaven.

 Blessed be your names.

 May your kingdom come.

 May your will be done, on earth as it is in heaven.

 Please give us our daily super-existential bread, and

 Please forgive our debts, as we forgive those who owe us.

 Please bless us with your light so we can be liberated from temptation and from evil.

May your kingdom and glory reign eternally on Earth."

"So be it."

INTERVENTION

Many of my children deprive others of free-will. Attempting to control outcomes. Thinking that they are doing the right thing for the greatest good. This is far from the truth. I want all my children to listen. Sometimes love disrupts. Sometimes it is fear tricking you with false safeties. In this chapter can you share with us the intervention that just happened in *your* life. Impacting you greatly.

To navigate through this depth, my child, it is essential that we transition out of gender polarity and into the sacred union with what is below.

We have explored the relationship with the masculine: All the dominant traits that you developed. The constant fighting to assert dominance and not be dominated. The systematic avoiding of *your* feelings. The deep untrust toward other men's intentions, as you do not trust your own. All that you forged to protect *yourself* from the terrifying perception that you had inherited towards men. All the thick and righteous walls that have been built between you and men to feel protected. Discovering an isolated and fearful *sacred heart*, aching for true connection.

We have also explored the relationship with the feminine: All the insecurities and urges that you have experienced. Putting women up on a pedestal and not knowing how to surrender to the feminine force within. Choosing to push away and reject the feminine instead. All the deep and confusing sense of resentment and attraction towards the qualities of the feminine. The deep love and devotion to the pure flow of the feminine. Now, deepening in the sacred journey, to find the wounded feminine within, hiding behind spells of confusion, seduction and possession.

Now, we will explore the sacred union that I AM:
Now, my child, we are in the deep waters, Ready to swim through the original separation within you. This story is ancient and speaks into the intense fears below.
To continue this journey, it is time to ground yourself into the unity of all things. To become the container for greatness!

"You are the container and the container is you."

The body is many bodies.
　　　Based on your own cosmic vision. The container, for you, is the most expensive and safe container that you can truly embody in wholeness.

In the centre of the centre. Starting inside the core of your seed. Inside, below all things and stories. There you will feel the source of innocence. Its purity has been corrupted, making you think that you have separated from the source. You can feel the pain of this separation. You can witness the still and breathless presence of the *anti-spirit* wanting to take your breath away. Seeking to trick you out of your existential power, so it can convince you of the need for its deceit.

This is designed for you to understand all your options. It is created for you to have the inner power of focus, stillness, determination and clarity. Key attributes to conquer your limiting perceived demons and to experience true *free-will*.

As you connect the vital and singular essence from the seed with above and below. In one single easeful breath or motion. You will flow directly to the sacred heart that has already been opened and stabilised. Receiving the light, in codes, from heaven. The subtle codes for greatness.

To stabilise, *bow down* the mind's eye to the greatness below. Breathe **this vital energy**, through your feet, to the core of *your* sacred mother below.

If this experience is new to you or if you don't feel whole right now and present. Please stop reading and breathe these codes into *your* heart. Continue reading until the sacred heart, in you, tells you to continue.

卍

As you navigate the deep oceans of being, dear beloved, polarity doesn't serve you anymore. You can't be consciously walking with two legs on different frequencies and realities. As you can't also be swimming deeply and still fighting the old fight between me and who you call Satan. It doesn't serve you anymore to have any sense of separation.

In this depth, union is essential to continue transcending. Union between thoughts and emotions. Union between the higher and the lower. Union between the inner and the outer. Union between *your* ancestral lineages and you. Union between man and woman. Union is when, in presence and breath, it all becomes one. Take a breath.

All that has been created in *your* life, it has been *your* choice. All in the spirit of discovering, healing and embodying who you truly are as I AM. All the thoughts of separation in the *shape* of competition, in the *shape* of romance, in the *shape* of needing to prove *yourself*, all these *shapes*, separate you from me.

All these thoughts are from the *shapes* interacting with each other. This back and forth has only created anxiety. Over time, you have been telling *yourself* that "you are not good enough exactly as you are." Stuck inside the world of comparing *shapes*. Lacking and *needing* to go outside. To the *shapes* and accomplish something to prove to *yourself* that you are worthy of value. This is not how a man is built, my child. All the internal fight, you have allowed, The original fight is with me, and it is only *taking* vitality out of you.

It takes away *your* presence, *your* peace and *your* love. All that you are in truth. This is why, right now, you are in a deep process of surrendering. Giving it all back to me. Remember, child, these moments of *your* life are also *your* choice.

The heaviness in *your* shoulders is from all the choices that you have taken, proving *yourself* to yourself that is the same as I AM. Y*our* father, on earth and in heaven. All the choices of carrying the *burden* of being on *yourself*. This is not your burden but mine. Please feel free right now, to take a deep breath and release this inherited load as you desire.

The tightness in *your* hips is from all the choices you have made of feeling guilt and shame from *your* deepest desires carrying density. It is in this space where we store all the emotions that we don't have the ability to process. It is time, dear one, to liberate the deepest truths of being. This space can get very tight if we are not living in a natural flow with the earth and the heavens.

The leaking from *your* groin is from all the choices you have made of fuelling sexual fantasies with women that you can set *your* eyes on. This way you avoid feeling the uncomfortable sensations that you are actually meant to be experiencing for *your* transcendental growth. No matter how innocent these fantasies can seem, dear child. No matter how righteous the masking of the shame and guilt can make you feel.

They are still illusions that separate you from me, from the love that you are and from your own greatness.

This battling and leaking energy has also been weakening *your* lower energy centres. Putting extra pressure onto *your* shoulders, neck and chest. This lack of certainty, as a man, not knowing who you really are in the core. It has trapped you into the illusion that the man that you are, is dependent on the woman that is by *your* side, and on *your* accomplishments in society. Dear one, you are not alone.

Now you know this. Most men and women are trapped in this illusion and are prisoners of this reality of external validation. Most on earth are trapped in the modern simulation that has been created by a phew for the many. However, knowing really doesn't make a difference or does it, my child? It only fuels the battle.

A breathing and open presence is how you can dissolve it. How you perceive *yourself* and *your* intention in the moment, permeates deeply into *your* internal rhythm. The decision of identity, in the now, affects all of the body. *Your* sacred energy is continuously permeating into every space in the *container* that is also known as the *somatic body*. Identity *shapes* the sacredness in you. How you name *yourself* impacts *your* breath, thoughts, sensory perceptions and the subtleties inside of how you walk. It impacts all that is You. It also impacts me and it impacts creation.

How you breathe, walk and observe does make a real difference to *your* energy field. It impacts *your* life greatly, dear one. The body that is in alignment with itself can easefully connect with its environment. Thank you, my dearest, for staying strong inside of I AM. *Your channel is clear.* Can you also see that it is not sustainable for you, as you are, without a true connection with our mother?

A true connection with the ancient wisdom below *your* feet, and with all the forms around you, happens through our mother. She is present on earth as I AM. Feel her. It is through the mother that you get to know me, *your* father in heaven. That I AM in you.

This is how you meet creation on earth, dear one. Through a deep connection with the mother. This is what has been missing for you, my child. If this is not resonant, thank you dear one! I ache, in the sacred heart, because most of my children are without deep roots to receive the mothers' support and nurture. Lacking, so many of my children drift and lose themselves again to the matter in time.

My child, please share with us the intervention that just happened through you. This is another moment in *your* growth, where *everything* around you imploded and shuffled for the greater good.
What happened?
How did it all start?

"It was December 2023 and it felt as if we, as a group, had reached the place of dreams. I was part of this beautiful romantic relationship with a beloved that met the depth of presence and expansiveness that I feel. We were also both part of this powerful *tribe* of like minded humans.

We were becoming a *known* tribe in the area. Our strong bonds, centeredness and clarity of heart was quite visible to the others. People around us were gravitating towards us and wanting to be a part of our group. *Especially* gravitating to heavenly music that a dear brother was able to receive and communicate.

Like minded humans were looking for leadership in the area. This perception was strong in their eyes. Inside of the dreaming of spirit. We are all seeking the same creations. Community, natural living, spiritual devotion, and off-grid abundance. It appeared that we had embodied more of these values, and this was giving us a magnetic pull of leadership.

Inside of *the tribe,* on the other hand, we were facing many cracks amongst us. We were embodying so much presence and light but in the depths of truth, commitment between us was not clear and we were not facing the truth of our demons. Inside our deep and dark vulnerability, we were really not sharing and holding each other in our ugly depths, for real, in love.

Most of us didn't know our depth yet. So most of us were getting quite light headed and ungrounded. Some of us were feeling *important* and significant by these leadership roles. Some of us were feeling uneasy that we were not sharing the *real* depths. Some of us were feeling insecure that we were not creating commitment, and many of us were jumping to conclusions, or we were simply confused about what was happening."

In the essence of humanity, dear one, nothing *special* was happening. The human experience is the same outside for all of you. Essentially, inside what arises in *your* own group dynamics, it is perfectly designed for all of you to show up to be seen and witnessed. The *good*, the *bad* and the *ugly*. In this essence the only *distinction* is that *your* lifestyle choice magnifies and speeds up the human experience, as you all go through the *veil of illusion*.

Regardless of what was happening, inside of this *tribe* you were still called up by the great mystery to lead the way. It was the end of 2023 and you received a call from a *landowner* inviting you to their land and co-create. At that moment, it was clear that it was time for *the tribe* to show up for the greater community around. The vision to vocalise a *Rainbow Gathering* in that land, became clear, so you did. Hundreds in the rainbow gathering conversation were keen to gather but no one had been able to find a suitable land, until now!

"It is relevant to the times to clarify that this particular rainbow movement is based on ancient prophecies of unity. It is not the ancient fight for inclusion that has started, in modern times, using the rainbow flag. This is another *false flag* movement promoted by mass media. The same machinery that seems to love creating and promoting labels that only want to separate us."

You are about to discover the depth of self-loathing, my child. The deep fight that exists in the body of humanity hurting us inside and out, and allowing for this machinery of separation to exist.

"This rainbow movement is based on the ancient rainbow serpent prophecies that described the *new earth*. How the leaders of the *new world* would come together, as a rainbow, representing **all the tribes**. The Rainbow Gathering is a decentralised social healing experiment that has been happening continuously around the world, for more than fifty years. As the saying inside the rainbow movement goes, 'there is a rainbow happening, somewhere, right now.'

Essentially, a group of people discover and secure a remote land in nature. A land that has enough clean water and where we have permission to come together in the hundreds, sometimes in the thousands.

Once the land is secured, the gathering is *vocalised* and the invitation spreads from heart to heart. The rainbow *family* is invited to arrive in the new moon and we build a village from nothing. Coming together for the collective healing in our planet.

We live together on this land for a month. Together we build a kitchen, toilet-pits and spaces for music, arts and tea. We create a central sacred fire that remains lit for the entire duration of the gathering. It is around this sacred fire where we come together to share food twice a day, dance and pray.

For this particular Rainbow Gathering, we came together next to a National Park and pristine waterfalls in the central east coast of Australia. A land worth to remember. In this instance we, as a tribe, were the *seeders* for this gathering. Essentially we were part of the small group who found the land, and started building the village two weeks before the big groups arrived."

It is beautiful to witness this much love in action from above. It was a particularly wholesome experience for you to be part of the *seed camp*. It felt like a full circle. After attending a number of rainbow gatherings, seeding offered a much deeper sense of connection and presence that comes from taking responsibility.

Then the social experiment started and it was very different to be in a core leadership position. You start receiving many *projections* from others' wounds. Reacting to a sense of authority, and reacting to their relationship with a masculine authority figure. You learnt a lot from these interactions.

It is a very expansive and challenging experience to be in a leadership position of a *Rainbow Gathering*. Particularly because it is attracting an external layer of humanity that is purposely responding against the many centuries of hierarchical masculine doctrine. Promoting instead the ancestral way of life, that is coming back in community.

This is what you signed up for, dear one. For this

life, you have agreed as I AM, to show up in leadership, wherever you go and whomever you are with. In this instance, it was very different to the *type* of leadership that you have been used to.

Hundreds of people with big personalities and characters. A deep sense of collaboration, an open sense of love, a strong sense of anarchy, and a highly developed sense of listening. These are some key qualities of the rainbow culture.

As time goes, the 2024 Australian Rainbow Gathering was getting close to its popular halfway mark. The halfway mark that is the most sought out night of the month. The full moon party! We are deep into the full moon party. You and *your* close friends are holding a strong unity consciousness portal of song, and prayer around the fire and totem pole. Most people are dancing high with psychedelic medicine, and everyone is enjoying themselves and taking flight.

During this night, you were clearly advised by our spirit that I AM, on the next steps for you: 'Let go of *your* responsibilities in this gathering and take rest. It is time to go deep into *your* own healing, allow for someone else to step up into leadership.' This is exactly what you did.

Now, after the party, in this new internal and receiving space, you were allowing for *your* deep wounds to arise into the surface, and allowing *yourself* to intimately connect with others to unravel and give love to these wounds. The phenomena of *your* experience, at this point, was quite new for you. You were experiencing quite similarly to how you are feeling right now that you are about to publish this book.

Essentially, you are in the centre with spirit, feeling and healing. A place that you are used to and comfortable inside. However, this time it feels much deeper, it feels true in your *seed* and your heart feels ignited. At the time this was very promising.

You were connected through the mother to everything that was happening in the gathering on that land. All the stories, all the emotions and conversations were being felt by you, through the mother. Regardless, if you were by *yourself* in the forest. In this particular experience you had expanded to connect with the whole land through the mycelium of the earth. You could hear the main conversations through the air and you could feel the gathering flowing through you. You were in perfect harmony with *your* natural order. Your energy was as magnetic and expansive as it is right now.

At this point two main events unfolded that allowed for the trickster to take over this gathering, and bring forth confusion, judgement and separation amongst you. It was meant for you, and many, to face *your-self*, like never before.

Firstly, you connected again with a charismatic

and magnetic friend . A woman you met in the times when you and *your* dear beloved were going through a pregnancy termination, a couple of years back. During that time you and *your* dear beloved were pushing each other away, as you couldn't see eye to eye through this process. In the past you did not feel much depth with this friend. This time around, you were surprised in how deep and powerful the connection was with her.

This was felt by anyone that you have a soul connection with, who was in the gathering. It was however interpreted by their own perceptions. You were indeed confused in *your* heart but knew that you would find clarity again, by going through it. *Your* dear beloved felt this, you spoke and she gracefully faced her own insecurities. She was deeply confronted by witnessing the depth of this connection. However, your commitment and devotion was with her.

Your close *brothers* saw this connection and, righteously, interpreted that you had lost the centre, again. In their perception, you were lost and *falling* in love like a puppy dog, without discernment. This perception was validated from *your* actions in the past. Particularly, when you moved out of the city, completely uncentered, you were falling in love with a different medicine woman every week.

Even though you were dealing with this connection with utmost integrity, unravelling it with presence and truth. Completely honouring *your* current sacred relationship. This happening, did create a wedge of doubt and judgement between you, and *your* closest ones. This perception got stuck in their psyche out of their own masculine wounding. The common wound amongst you that makes it more comfortable for others to be viewed smaller and pigeon holed in the mind, rather than being witnessed in their true greatness.

Regardless, a noticeable wedge between you and *your* loved ones was happening. This separation was bringing forth the perceptions of division amongst you. The perceptions from the trickster. The perceptions of power. The perceptions of judgement and fear. It was only a matter of time for something to break down.

In *your* heart, you could witness all of this happening but you were trusting in its impermanence and that *your* intimate and trusted ones had your back and would hold unity in their hearts. You were trusting in the deep and strong bonds amongst you.

Secondly, in the rainbow gathering there was a big event about to erupt. Suddenly an older man spoke up, and declared that he was a *convicted paedophile*, that's right, we are going there. I know that this can be very confronting. Remember to breathe with me. This conversation happened as *by law* he had to let everyone know because there were kids in the gathering. In this particular rainbow gathering there were dozens of young kids. This became a major issue for most. Specially, parents in their natural protector roles would not have a bar of this discussion.

Parents wanted to expel this man immediately,

and some people even destroyed his belongings. The worst fears and prejudice from humanity was showing up. Symbolically, this man was being sought by the masses with *pitchforks*. A number of young wounded men saw the opportunity to feel as men, and unconsciously jumped up to the *protector* roles. They started to rally around wanting to kick this man out immediately. As normal as this might sound in the world, this is not the spirit of the Rainbow Gatherings. Can you speak into this, dear child?

"In Rainbow Gatherings we recognise that we are inside these collective wounds together. We are encouraged to work through them by sitting together, in a circle of peace, and listening to each other. This way we can find a deeper understanding of the moment, and the opportunity to face and heal our fears, and wounds.

This is the rainbow family way and the ancestral ways. This is how we find, as a community, a higher perspective. This is the way to listen to each other and discover an agreement forward, where we are all being met.

That day the spirit was very loud asking me to find this circle, and join. It felt that *my* presence was going to be relevant to reach a higher place of healing. This particular circle of peace felt very important to the cosmic fibres of creation. It felt like transcendental times were upon us. We were healing the seed of innocence. The core of the *cosmic spiritual battle* that we are all a part of, was at play: **The corruption of the innocent.**

For thirteen hours we sat in a circle. The

convicted paedophile was present the whole time, listening, justifying and taking on the messages of growth. I was speaking from compassion and higher truth. Many in the circle were speaking, understandably, from fear and prejudice.

For me in particular, I was riding a deep and powerful wave of healing within *my* seed. I was holding a space for all present to drop the act, feel the vulnerability and have a look inside. Hoping to be able to breathe love back to our own seed of innocence.

Indeed, I led that conversation to reach the core of its truth. Together we found a way where we all felt comfortable in its conclusion. An agreement was found. No one was being kicked out, and the healing of all involved would continue until the end of the gathering.

This man, in the present moment, was not doing anything to hurt anyone. However, in the present he still had fantasies with the young ones. It was clear from this that he could not be part of the gathering anymore, and that we needed to protect the children. From this line on the sand, we looked for an agreement together.

After hours of listening, expressing and feeling a lot of emotions. We all agreed that he was going to stay on the land but he was going to move to the edge of the land where he was not going to interact with any children. We agreed that two of us men will be with him at all times, as *chaperones* to provide safety for everyone. Two of us agreed to be by his side and we agreed that we would take food to him, so he wouldn't come across kids around the fire. He would stay on the land so he could finish the healing cycle that he was navigating, and continue being supported in this conversation inside further healing circles.

We agreed that we were going to hold a men and women's circle to continue going deeper into the healing of this fundamental collective trauma that shakes us all so much. To offer safety to everyone involved, myself and the other *chaperon,* we were going to hold space for this man to be present in the sharing circle.

We felt accomplished and ready for a good rest. After such a heroic day for many of us, we had reached unity in the depths of our beings. The next day came but there was another plan in the making. A plan that was happening and unravelling a different direction for all of us."

A couple of people in this sharing circle, where, at the time, somewhat attached with leadership and in being part of the tribe that you are a part of. Not out of ill intentions but from being rather young and ambitious to prove themselves. What you witnessed is that It was as if you were in high-school all over again. You were part of the *cool group* that everyone wanted to be a part of, and all the politics that happened around this hierarchical perception of belonging and perceived power. At that time, it felt for you that it was key for them to be seen as powerful protectors for the gathering, regardless. They were forcing through the perceptions of the *protector* archetypes, even though, collectively, you had the capacity to not react, and create a new precedent to the situation.

Suddenly, that morning, before the announcements, they had spoken in tones of emergency to *your* closest brothers, with the alarming message that you were not fit. You were not to be trusted and you must be stopped before the announcements. Our dear brothers, dealing with their own, did fall into this *trickery*. There was not such noise going on at the time. Rather, what existed where lies from the unconscious wounds, and echoes from the past that needed to be dealt with.

Regardless, the intervention happened. You were blindsided to join them before the announcements, and actually received by a *hostile and casual intervention*. Surrounded by two of *your* close and trusted brothers, a new brother that you are just learning to understand, unmask and trust, and by the two younger ones that were being used by their own ambitions.

You were not in a circle of trust. Inside this irresponsible container, the intervention became a very messy, explosive and sticky situation. This was an intervention that interrupted all *your* relationships.

An intervention that told you four main things that they were concerned about. Four points that were not entirely true but later did offer you, in *your* name, inside *your* own learning and transcendance, the same gold that is meant for you.

1. "I was not fit to hold a mens circle that day because I was trauma bonding with the paedophile. This, as I was also abused as a child."
2. "I was not fit to vocalise and be seen as a leader in the gathering, because *some women* in the gathering didn't trust me to hold this sacred space of healing. It was passionately expressed that one woman felt unsafe and had left the gathering because of me having a leadership position."
3. "I was not fit to vocalise a mens circle because my communication skills were not good, as I was not able to speak concisely and to the point."
4. "I was not fit to lead the tribe to create a community. This as I speak with business/sales language and this was confusing to external people, and *pushing* people away."

This *intervention*, my child, did not come from love and compassion but rather from fear and judgments. It created an immediate short circuit in *your* system and you exploded as a lion explodes when falsehoods are attempting to take over the sacred space. You were cornered in force to accept this perception. You growled and you left this attempt to intervene with your free-will. You knew, without a doubt, that what was being spoken was not true but something else was playing out.

For the remainder of the day you could not hold yourself out of the child 's position. Your closest were still in the *high horse spell* and could not see the unravelling. You ran into them and expressed your disgust. This sparked another emergency circle later in the evening to hold you now with all of your trusted brothers. You received this act of love and this allowed you to rebuild. However, inside that circle, you had no filters, and your closest brothers still spilled onto you their perceptions and agendas.

For the next two months, without much other options, you were alone and in stillness for the most part, discerning what happened. You reached out and spoke heart to heart with almost everyone involved to clarify and get to the bottom of this mess.

You uncovered the truth and saw clearly all the wounds that people around you were covering up for themselves, and some still are. The important aspect for you is that *your* close brothers did have an important message to offer you.

You also discovered, six months later, a deeper hurt in this unmasking. Essentially, the woman who *apparently* vocalised, leaving the rainbow gathering because she didn't feel safe around you. Turned out to be made up. It all came from the unseen wound of someone pushing her own agenda.

There are no accidents. The wounded nature of this particular one, manipulating views and pushing through an agenda, is here to show you a deeper perspective of *your* own mothers' ways. You are able to see her now much clearer, my child. In fact, you are now very proud of *your* work during the years. This woman in question, who allegedly didn't feel safe around you. You spoke with her, In deep humility. She acknowledged that she has been witnessing you, and she is quite proud of the work that you have been doing over the years. She left the gathering because she had to go, and it was nothing to do with you.

Regardless, of all these discoveries, and all that has been transmuted and transcended. It has been particularly hard to *shake off* this experience. The *timing* and *shapes* of this *intervention* was not coming from love but rather from fear disguised as care.

It was not an *accident* but rather it was the *tricksters'* doing. After many of you left the back door of consciousness unattended. It was important to stop the creation of a new conversation. A new example on how to deal with the *horrific* wounding of child abuse. It is clear now in the present, my child.

Now that you have uncovered all the *energetics* and the space in your heart. It is again whole and at ease. The hurt has been acknowledged by most, and the shadows are clear to be seen. Now it is when forgiveness and compassion, will show you the way back to love. In perfect timing you will come back full circle, with all your dear beloved.

"The agenda of the wounded masculine is very clear for me to see nowadays. We have been describing it also throughout this book. The force. The fight. The Walls. The stubborn mind. The lies from personality. The pressure to prove ourselves. It is much easier to be a witness of these qualities. The masculine within, feels much safer in the *physical domain* and prefers to push out the wounds and be more *physical* in the *phenomena* of the healing process.

These events, on the other hand, reminded me of how the agenda of the wounded woman within, has also been manifesting through the collective subconscious. The womb that is still feeling deeply unsafe in *our world*, and hides behind chaos and uncertainty. The one that seeks to possess and control the heart of men through subtle energetic manipulations. The agenda that wants to create a matriarchal system and replace the patriarchy. The agenda that prefers for men to be emasculated and be *good boys*, to feel safe, and in line with women's leadership.

All of the historical reactions ignited by our instinct for survival and evolution, and fuelled by our deepest fears. Are we going to be able to reset? Are we going to be able to re-wild? Are we going to be able to come back home? Are we going to open, and allow ourselves to be authentically guided by love?"

This is true, dear one. These reactionary agendas come from *your* ancestral wounding and they are not allowing the creation of sacred union within you These reactionary agendas keep many of you going around in circles. It is time now, my children, to fulfill on what you truly deserve. No more hierarchical and reactionary systems. It is time for the sacred union within to show us the way forward!

Indeed, I am so proud of you, dear one.

You listened, and listened, and listened for the truth. Through this deep contemplation you have picked up the *gold* from this intervention.

- You recognise that from *your* fear of belonging, you have been melowing *yourself* for others to feel more comfortable. This has limited the fire in *your* expression. It is this fire that is being called for by creation. No more holding back, my child.

- You recognise that you have been leaking sexual energy, Still holding sexual fantasies in the depths of *your* system and suppressing them. You recognise feeling shame and guilt for being a sexual being. This judgement has been holding you back. These undertones have been creating all of the untrust that you have been suffering from *your* environment. It is time to completely contain the energy of this vessel, and to empty *yourself* from judgement. Allow to be exactly as you are. Allow yourself to express your desires. It is not healthy for you to keep quiet.

- You recognise that you are surrounded by what mainstream culture labels as *hippies*, and business/marketing language confronts them, inside their own inherited wounding. It is important to be generous, patient, offer context, and simplicity of language, always.

- You recognise that you and others have been attached to the concept of *tribe* and not really looking and accepting *your* own wounds. Feeding into spiritual egos. Attached to a certain outlook, rather than walking faithfully and committed, into the unknown. It is clear, for me, that I want you to be realised and not trapped into any-*thing*. Even if it may sound and look beautiful to the senses.

For eight months, after that date, you have gone through so many trials and tribulations, my beloved. You have brought back crystal truth. It was so impactful for you that there was no other way. It was by speaking with everyone involved that allowed you to understand what actually happened, and allowed you to be able to develop compassion for *yourself,* and for others, who did not act from the centre of truth.

For six months, you have been mainly walking alone. Meeting many people outside of the closer circles that you are a part of. You have been calling in more realness and less spiritual bypassing through the beauty of words. You have been calling in more ancient roots and culture, with less convenient ideas coming from *western culture*. You have been calling in more *condors* around you. More people, from the cultures of the *south* that intrinsically know the ways of the heart and community.

You have been calling in new bonds and relationships that are crystal clear. Intimate soul connections that are clear in its commitment and clear in the roles within. You are calling for the people closest to you to have the courage to show up at their worst. As the self worth to show up at their best.

As you conclude to write this section, you are still feeling anger and distrust coming through. The feeling of betrayal becomes the main fuel wanting to hijack you from the centre that I AM. You continue to unravel this drama, and bring it back to the love that I AM.

Your bonds with tribe members are becoming clearer. Then again it is not as you were thinking but rather, a new depth of being that is further detached from illusion is arising. Anger and distrust is still present in *your* energy field, and it is perfect, my child.

You cannot force relationships to be. For love to happen and blossom, we need to create space and time in between the forms. The forms disappear with our allowance that comes through our forgiveness. This is when unconditional love, where I AM, is possible for you. It becomes gracefully present when you can be in-love, where there is no form, this is the true meaning of love.

You are witnessing rage at *your* most intimate friends and beloved. You are angry for pretending to be an embodied truth, rather than showing up inside the truth of vulnerability. You can see them being confused as well, being utilised by the archetypes that want to keep us in the shadows. Particularly the archetype of the carer and protector.

Can you also see that this is all you, dear child? Have you not also been pretending to be a man behind the caring protector? It is very common in *your* world. It is so common for wounded men and women to bypass healing, and find purpose in the roles that it has become hard to identify and witness. This is why there are so many walls and rules in human reality.

A wounded boy doesn't really know how to create true safety for women and children, without barriers and force. A wounded girl sees fear wherever she feels challenged. The protector, and other archetypes, are being used by the *trickster* to hide our wounds. Be vigilant. The protector is an easy step for the wounded boy and girl to feel like a man and a woman.

The protector is definitely needed, there are people that are very out of sorts that can be dangerous. Then again, is the protector vigilant and containing the events in the centre, or is the protector, out of the centre, rejecting any *risky* events from happening in the first place. The wounded protector is many times called forth from our own internal wounding. Yet, many times the healthy protector is called forth from clear intuition. It is a fine line to discern, my child. Are you responding or are you reacting?

Keep listening. This is a relevant conversion, as the accumulation of these wounded protectors, acting out of fear, creates a *fearful reality*. It is the force behind many men showing up and going to war, for example.

As you continue to recognise a deep wounding of betrayal, you also recognise the deep sense of care and commitment that you were holding for *the tribe* and its future is gone. You feel that you are actually not seen by this group and relationships cannot be forced. Most people on earth, dear beloved, conveniently perceive the big players through their limitations and agendas, instead of their greatness. This is another way for the mind to trick us into a false sense of greatness through comparison or the depreciation of others.

You are perceiving betrayal as a major wound dictating all of *your* relationships. This is perfect, my child. You can free *yourself* from any guilt that comes from feeling all these rejection, towards the people that you love the most. You are not alone, most human relationships are sitting on top of these repressed fears of not belonging and being rejected. Betrayal has been a common pattern amongst you for centuries. Let us discover and transmute this together.

Where did it start for you in this body, dear child?

"I feel an enormous sense of battle from betrayal with my older brother, as I was growing up. We were not loyal to each other. I feel an ancestral argument of competition for the favour of our mother playing out between us. It is an ancient drama that has nothing to do with him or me, as people, but rather it has to do with an ancient wound amongst men that is showing the limitations of our creation.

I sense a wound, in both of us, competing for our mothers' embrace and attention. I sense an ancient argument between men to gain the favour and the love from women. I am witnessing men, for lifetimes, competing for love through might, through manipulation and through casting shadows over other men. Thank you brothers for *your* vulnerability.

I can also feel and witness the wounded feminine. As it has played out, it is a reflection for me of what exists within my mother's *lineage*. I hadn't been able to observe this. Many generational blockages were in the way. The freedom of new generations has given me the ability to witness these deep patterns. Thank you sisters for *your* courage. Regardless, I feel so angry for this dynamic of betrayal happening, time and time again in this lifetime. I am witnessing that the bright light that I AM, does confront other men and activates this deep wounding. I let go of trying to understand this deep feeling of betrayal. I will continue to witness and transcend as I AM. I love my brothers and I will come back to love as much as I can."

卐

My child, *your* lack of humbleness towards the great light in you, could have been the trigger in them. No one wants to be left without their own light. Our attention, our affection and our conviction makes it so. Betrayal has been a theme for you, my child. Being betrayed by lovers with dear friends. Being betrayed by dear friends with lovers, and being betrayed to gain business. Being betrayed by the closest to you so they can gain favour and light.

You are not alone, my child. Betrayal is an ancestral wound that we have been healing from the beginning of time. Ever since the sense of separation and scarcity were validated to be true. We felt a sense of threat from the greatness of another. The relevant thing for you to discover is, where have you betrayed others' trust? and, where have you betrayed your own trust!? It is in this betrayal that you are creating the betrayals of others to be real in *your* existence.

Beloved dear child, you have also been unfaithful to *your* sacred relationships. However, most of *your* betrayal has been covert. Secretly desiring success and love, at the expense and demise of another. Although you didn't take the actions most of the time, the vibrations were in existence in *your* life and playing themselves out. You have kept the story of betrayal alive in the body by holding onto all these angry sensations, from being a teenager. Deeply repressed in *your* underbelly.

Old story lines that are full of fear and despair, carrying feelings of unfaithfulness and jealousy towards *your* closest friends and beloved. This is what has kept betrayal alive in *your* connections. You have not completed this circle of development. The full circle that becomes alive for most of you during your late twenties.

"May you free yourself from anything and everything that is not pure love as I AM."

As you observe with your gaze, you are blessing creation. As you look and take a snapshot to understand that moment, or this moment, you are condemning creation to become of that particular view. This is the true power that you are, dear one. Each one of you.

"I write on a park bench, next to a children's playground. Parents there are suspicious and protective. 'What is this guy doing here alone next to our kids?' So I think! In truth, I am deep in the challenges of healing the root of the matter. The same that I like to describe as the corruption to my kundalini essence. Children's energy is supporting me to remember this. At this point in time, I am healing so deeply, inside the deep oceans, that the collective sexual wound is being seen and coming out to be seen by others. This is triggering others around me as well. It is all part of the healing process. The abuse of the innocent is the core of the deep corruption that has formulated our societies.

I am restoring this innocence for myself. Child abuse is what I am dealing with. These are the fibres, within that I am healing in this lifetime. These are the wounds that have infected our innocence and birthright with the divine."

Yes, beloved child. In the practical human experience *your* sexual energy has been leaking out of *your* body ever since you were sexually abused as a boy. Now that you are in a very deep place healing, this profound experience is leaking out of *your* body and others are picking up on that.

This is really good, my child. To heal we need to feel, and to feel we need to reveal! This energy that you are feeling now is creating scenarios that are testing you. Testing to see if there are any reactions that will validate you being outside of the centre that I AM. Testing to see if you are ready to be true to all that you are, or if you are still meant to be living through the stories of humanity.

Men confronting you out of the woods are being fueled by their own fears and wounding. Testing you, in an attempt to bring doubt back into *your* mental space. All these tests are fuelled by *your* own shadows. You are facing untrue rumours attempting to spread into the physical. My child, nothing is outside trying to get you. These rumours are fueled by the echoes in *your* subconscious. The echoes from the wounded masculine and the wounded feminine, wanting to be unveiled.

These are the echoes that come from not fully trusting *yourself*. Trust, my child. You are healing.

It is time, child, to go deeper into *your* wounding. Please feel deeper. Here is where *your* darkest desires are being distracted. These are the waves of dissidence holding you back from being in harmony with nature. I want you to practise being in a surrendered *child pose*. In this place I want you to tighten the navel and *your* thighs. Breathe into the depths of *your* being. Feel the depth of *your* vulnerability and desire.

This practice is called Mula bandha, it means *locking the root chakra*. Mula bandha is the yogic practice of drawing the root chakra up and in. The root chakra is said to be located at the base of the torso, or the perineum.

> Feel the sensations below *your* navel, the sensation in *your* thighs and narrow them into the sensations in *your* anus.

> Feel all the subtle sensations there and all the sensations that you felt in getting there. Be attentive to all the blockages and new openings that show up in *your* spine.

> Feel the amount of energy that is stored there, in *your* root. Feel the deep desire of connection that lives there. Be there as long as it is

comfortable. Breathing the sensations upwards into *your* heart.

Breathe through it all…

Beloved child, do you feel how these anxious sensations creep down *your* thighs? Can you feel that they influence how you walk? Can you see that they also influence where you end up walking towards?

Let these sensations be. Let them go through you and give them back to the mother sustaining you. These anxieties accumulate everyday, every day there is a world of unprocessed and unwarranted sensations that come through us. May you have a daily practice to observe all these sensations and give them back to the mother.

You are not alone, beloved child. These sensations make most of the personalities archetypes that many men and women are trapped into. Now that you have progressed, quite a bit, in distinguishing the subtle sensations of *your* body, you can do this deeper work. You have already conquered many feelings of guilt, shame and prejudice that used to imprison the sacral energy in you. Now you can navigate in these deep waters. Now you are free to be inside of *your* sexual energy. You are free to ride this powerful force and choose who and what you give *your* desire of creation to.

Choose with *your* breath. Be gentle. Feel it all. There are many sensations of guilt, shame and prejudice that you haven't yet uncovered, my child.

There are many sensations of lack that are seeking connection, and seeking validation that are still alive in you. Feel it all, my child. You will find the stillness deep within the pleasure, below all things.

Breathe it all. Below all things you will find the presence that I AM. Below all things you can feel the connection with The Sacred Mother, my beloved. Giving and receiving, with you, at *your* root base. Be with my beloved. Get strong below, my child. Let go of all the desires that don't serve you. Let go of all the desires that take away peace from *your* heart. Our eternal union *awaits* in the heart. Exactly where I AM waiting for you.

You are the miracle, my child. You are not alone. You are the one that brings together the heavens and earth. It all happens in *your* heart centre. The invitation is to stay curious within. Stay with my beloved, *your* mother, and get strong. The root is an energy centre that you have not yet activated. Connect with what is below. An abundant tree is held by its deep and healthy roots.

Keep Breathing

    I AM that I AM

        Keep Breathing

            I AM that I AM

                Keep Breathing

                    I AM that I AM

卐

I am very proud of you, my child. It has not been an easy process to heal the depth of *your* soul. These depths are 'out of bounds,' for many on earth. Most simply don't have access to them. Thank you for sharing *your* light. During these times, the wounding has been out in the open and you have been singled out by mobs on the street. You have been accused of being a pervert. You have been accused of being a danger to women and children. Who is accusing you?

"Other men that have not had the stomach to deal with their own wounding."

Can you see the deception of illusion amongst mankind? Most on earth are simply reflecting back their own suppressed fears and wounds. Pretending that they are *good boys* and *good girls*. In fact, you are all dealing with the same ancestral mess that is holding humanity down. I am very proud that you are holding the higher truth alive, my child. The truth of healing all the separation between us. The truth that we are in this together. You have been singled out in *your* healing because most people do not bring up to the surface the depth of the sexual wounding that mankind is facing. This can be very confronting for the many.

You are now reaching the light at the end of this tunnel. You are feeling a lot stronger below. A lot more centred and clear of who you are in the core, as I AM.

There is a golden key that you have found in this process. You have been very studious, my child. Understanding new feelings that you had not allowed *yourself* to be aware of and feel. Particularly, the feeling of despair. Do you want to share more about this experience, my child?

"So much has opened up for me. I have allowed myself to be in stillness and to feel the strong sensation of despair. This has shifted so much of my perception. I realised that by not allowing myself to feel despair, I was operating on top of this sensation, from an anxious space. Resisting and not feeling these strong sensations. I realised how much of *my* impatience and inability to be at peace, came from not allowing *myself* to feel despair."

This is so beautiful, my child.
    Can you recognise that there is no other way for you to feel hope, in its fullness, unless we allow ourselves to feel the opposite first? The opposite being the experience of despair. Can you recognise that *your* hope, up until this point, has also been existing together with this anxious space? This is not a wholesome way to connect with the power that I AM.
    The anxiety masking despair is how you have been hiding the deep fear of not existing. The deep fear of being lost. The deep fear of being abandoned. The

deepest fears of mankind are hiding underneath the strong sensations of despair. Allowing *yourself* to be in peace with despair, and allowing *yourself* to breathe freely through it. This is what allows you to be powerfully at peace with the unknown. Not-knowing is the truth, my child. Not knowing is when *your* mind has accepted with humility that it truly doesn't fathom creation. This is when we connect in spirit. This is when you accept *yourself* as a created being who is also blessed to be a creator. Can you see this with humility and a receptive heart?

"This is so true, I feel a void when I am disconnected from you. Immediately behind this void I feel strong sensations of despair, and a quick impulse to fill me up with external things or matter. This so I can stop feeling. An impulse to consume matter takes over me. Being this matter in the form of thoughts, food, substances, pretty objects, or pretty women to make me feel better."

This is very true, my child. When we get disconnected you are left to fence with creation *independently*. In *your* own will. This can be a mammoth experience to be confronted by. Instead, many of my children choose to get numbed down with consumption and not feel despair and the deep void underneath. This is not what I have created you for, my child. You deserve much more.

In my own will, as I AM, you are fulfilled with ease and grace. Filled with all blessings. When you surrender to my will, and allow for my will to be done. *Your* life becomes what we have dreamt for you, my child. Life gets filled and lifted up with the divine nectars of Hope, Faith and Love.

What is stopping you, my child, from surrendering as I AM?

"Everything that we have uncovered in this book is still present in my body and my mind. It is all still alive. I don't feel worthy of love.

I understand that I am love but I am not feeling it consistently. It is as if my mind and the memories from it, keep getting into my field and creating doubt or confusion. I keep searching for the one, for the one that I will mate with, and create life.

I make the effort to stay focused and keep surrendering but I keep distracting myself easily. I keep getting out of centre, getting hooked to netflix and women that I meet. Looking for distractions. There is nothing wrong with this. I know this. Yet I can witness that it takes me out of centre and the sacred connection with you."

It is not about *what* you are doing, dear one, it is about *how* you are doing it. What is the intention of the action that you are doing right now? You have *your* addictions and *your* distractions, dear beloved. Habits that don't make you feel proud of *your* days. Inside of this deep healing and surrender, you will find new ways.

Please don't be hard on *yourself* when you falter. Who can blame you? Who can judge you? We are all swimming in this profound sea of love. We all need *time* to rest. As the whales and dolphins play in the depths. The gift of joy is missing. This is what makes the whole experience in the deep to be easeful and enjoyable. It is in this place where we can reprogram together the fibre of creation that you have conditioned *yourself* into. Enjoy always. Dear child.

Many years, desiring the flesh of women. Many years feeling that you are not good enough. It has become such an automatic way for you to perceive creation and the beauty of women. These depreciating and sexualised neurological pathways have created deep grooves into the fabric of creation in you.

Now, you are clear that it is not serving you anymore. It is difficult for you to perceive differently and to do it consistently. You have hardwired this perception into the routine of your internal choices. It will take time and discipline to transform these pathways, my child. Keep surrendering to this work. Keep feeling deeply in stillness.

You don't know when the transformation, in its root, will occur. You do know that it will certainly happen and it will happen in the ease and grace that I AM. I promise you this to be so. You are receiving guidance, keep listening, my child. Stay true to *your* vulnerability. This is *your* strength. It is as it is, and it will continue to be so, my child. All that is, it is right here now. What is not here and now, it is creating life somewhere else but not in *your* presence. All the winds of desires. All the expansions of truth and all the contractions from fear. It is all coexisting now. It is the discipline in *your* practice that makes you a true disciple or not.

The self in you, still lingers on the pleasure from the desires of the flesh. It makes you feel alive. You are addicted to feeling the vitality that comes from sexual arising, my child. You simply love the feeling of aliveness and feeling desired. As we all do. In this reality you are yearning to be validated and to feel alive. Yearning to be softened inside the embrace of love. Yearning to feel the full embrace of acceptance. Yearning to feel the activation of sex.

If you wish, surrender this illusion, my child. In the truth of creation, you are love. You are accepted as you are and you are truly alive! Can you see that it is only you who can give these blessings to *yourself*?

Reality, by definition, is nothing more than *your* relationship with *things*. Reality is completely relative, and you have the power to choose *your* own reality. You were created free, and it is *your* perception, created by *your* thoughts and emotions, that gives rise to the *reality* that you are experiencing. Continue to unravel the reality that you have been choosing and be free to choose newly as you will. May the beauty of the I AM that AM find its way to all of *your* senses.

Great work, my child.

    I am seeing more of you in the depths of *your* being. I am seeing more light of truth in *your* legs and *your* steps. Keep walking in this light. Everyday walk in truth and the blessings will multiply. *Your* intention of becoming one as a creator will only continue to grow. You are my son and *your* mother carries you to me. You are not alone, my child. May you always remember this.

    The sexual perversion of men and women is an ancient poison, my child. Most people have the same, only suppressed behind clouds of shame and guilt. Thinking that this is the right thing to do. Thinking that it is best to keep it all hidden inside the bottomless pit that is the body. Then again the consequences of these suppressed feelings are pervasive in all of society. Anger and frustration is amongst you. Infidelity to the sacred truth, and, the insatious, lack of power within prevails. All of this only creates amongst you impatience, invalidation and untruthful dynamic systems.

    Thank you my child, for *your* courage to go through the shame and the guilt. To uncover the pervasive and corrupted sexual energies within. This will only give you further strength, presence, peace and the ability to create like no other. May you continue this blessed, and sacred, path that you have chosen. We have always been one.

"I am inside the choice of creating conscious presence in my legs and feet. I am feeling the deep realms of perversion of my ancestors that I AM. I am faced with demons that I have seen before many times in myself, and others.

I am faced with my own perversions from this lifetime. My choices when I was a teenager. The choices of masturbation and pornography. The choices of going out to the nightlife as much as I did. Only to charm and seduce women and satisfy urges of manhood. I am faced with waves of anger, waves of possessive desire, and waves of shame"

Can you truly forgive *yourself*?

Now, you are leaving this prelude. At the time you felt completely separate. Separate from you and separate to all around you. It is deep into the program that you learnt and repeated many times.

Reel ALL of *yourself* back in. Reel ALL of *yourself* back into the body, my child! Hold *your* legs together and contain our energy. Breathe the sacred centre that I AM. Bathe in it as much as you desire. Use this space to create *your* deepest heart's space and be able to create freely. *Your* deepest desire was to be ONE with me as I AM, and to be in complete freedom. Is this still the case?

"Yes. These are my deepest desires."

You are free from *your* bondages, my child. You are blessed amongst the many. You are a true free man. Living with purpose. Working and communicating with love. We will become all one. This I can promise. You are living the times that humans have sang and preached about through the ages. The *second coming,* the *end of times.* In the East there is a story called the era of *Kali Yuga.* This is now also coming to its end. An era of cleansing. An era where women are on the cusp of becoming fully empowered through the generations. Able to be more bold in cutting down the heads of men. All of this, for men to be humbled and heart centred. Praying deep in the fabric of creation for the heart of men to become crystal.

"Praying for a crystal field to be held, for our unique sacredness to be safe."

It is all happening, my child.

Remember that it is very important to have crystal clear agreements in all *your* relationships. This is how the sacred heart thrives in creation. This is how we offer our relationships a steady and firm ground to expand from. Remember that when someone doesn't want to create a committed relationship. This person is not yet ready to manifest their own creation into existence. This person is still figuring out if they are real or not. After all, the root meaning of commitment is the agreement to make something happen and, as you know, nothing happens without an agreement. Remember that when you are looking for *home* outside of you. In the form of a woman, or any other worldly accomplishment. You are really looking to connect back home. The home that has always been exactly where you are. *Eighteen inches* below *your* head. Exactly here where I AM.

Breath it all in *yourself*, my child. It is all you. Breath all the different vibrations that make up creation. It is all you. The crisp highs. The dense lows. The drowning waters. The erupting volcanoes. It is all alive in you and it is all a dream but a deep sea of love. Feel settled inside the vibration that naturally exists in *your* presence. *Your* natural vibration of love. Feeling *your* particular love that is deep, wholesome, transparent, piercing and warm.

"Do you want to be in love or do you want to be right?"

It is when you are not feeling *your* loving energy field, my child, when we need to observe what is the story playing out in the mind where you are. What is the story, in time, that is taking us out from the eternal presence of love. Who is speaking to you when you hear this story within the mind? Is it ancestral? Is it in the collective? Is it *your* higher intelligence? Are these stories bringing you boldness of spirit or is *your* light being deemed?

It is a very fine line, dear child. Discernment and communication is key to be clear of this fine line of existence between the real and the unreal. Breathe. Discern what is and let it go. Breathe. This is the most important message for you. Breathe with me. All that is not peaceful, alive and nurturing. It is not the soothing energy of one. The energy of one is right there where you are. You are simply called to not do anything and breathe. I will show up, as I do, when there is the space, between *your* words, to do so.

When you sit in *your* own soothing breath. It all regulates back to its original natural flow of love.

"I AM this soothing breath of love."
Breathe. *Your* body is getting regulated.

"I AM this soothing breath of love."
Breathe. The three bodies are becoming one.

"I AM this soothing breath."
Breathe. I AM ONE.

"I AM this soothing breath."
Breathe I AM.

TRUSTING LOVE

"I am angry at myself. I feel, right now, so much cynicism towards love. Intense resignation that is not allowing me to connect to love authentically.

I feel angry at how beautiful people speak about love and spirit, and how much everyone is actually, hiding our true vulnerability and pretending that we have everything under control.

I feel frustrated at the fear of people, as I commit authentically to creation. I am tired of people using truth and the language of spirit to their convenience.

I am witnessing my body seeking to contract and validate the fears towards love. I am witnessing spirit continuously seeking its expansion. I am witnessing the battle of love and fear happening in me, right now.

I feel scared and a rebellious spirit wanting to check out as I breathe. Tired and desperate from the feelings of ache and insecurity in this heart. I am feeling like I want to quit on love.

I feel angry towards women for hiding behind chaos and manipulating love from there. I feel angry at men for pretending that they are ready to be in love when they are not. I feel angry towards myself for being in this condition again.

I feel angry that I am doubting love again. I am angry that I have not been able to hold myself worthy. I am angry that I am drowning with these pitiful emotions, outside of love."

" I breathe through all of this lack. As long as it takes. I trust in you, my creator that I AM. Please guide me back to love."

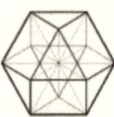

"I can recognise that by hurting myself, I am hurting everyone. I am recognising that if I continue to take myself out of action, and into depreciation, I validate my suffering and keep this suffering alive for myself and for everyone else. I can recognise the magnitude of this presence that I AM, or the lack of presence thereof, and how much it impacts the environment. I can see how everyone shows up differently, based on how I choose to show up. I can recognise that love is what uplifts me, holds me, and heals me. I can recognise that love is what I truly perceive to be the way and the truth. Love in all its frequencies, forms and expressions."

You are not alone, my child. These contrasts are very visible to you because of *your* depth of presence. This happens to every one of you, in case you haven't noticed, we are in this together. We will unravel the story of love that you are swimming in. May *your* waters be cleared and purified.

"Today I spoke over the phone with the woman that I was ten years married with. It feels so good to be able to listen to her and support her when I can. It feels good, now, to not feel responsible for her but to feel responsibility with her. It feels great to be able to empower the people that I love when I can.

I am very connected to her, I can feel her in my depth. I know that she is struggling. I know that it is not for me to walk with her. I pray for healthy ways in which I can support her. She is part of the love story of this body. This is true and it is honouring all that this body is. She is part of this presence, and she will be directly blessed through me. I am honouring her deep and devotional love. I am honouring her committed way of being. I am honouring her unwavering focus in sitting with the uncomfortable truth. I am honouring her beautiful love and commitment to taking care of her family and healing her ancestry.

As I love one thing, it is how I love everything else. As I love the passing breeze, as I love our neighbour, as I love our pets. Deep inside as I love one, I love *everything* else. Nothing in this creation is separate. We are in this together, all the way. Even if I cannot perceive this truth, yet.

For me, in particular, it is through romantic love that I am able to dive deeper into love and translate this new depth into all my relationships. Including the essential relationship with *myself*. As I learn to go deeper with another, this opens up my ability to love everything else in this new depth of existence.

However, through this life, I have not been in true

love. I have only had fleeting moments of this pure essence being sustained in a relationship. I have been close to sacred unconditional reciprocation. Yet, *my* self love hasn't allowed me to go further. Someone in the connection, closes the heart somewhat. Not able to receive or give the flow and intensity of pure love anymore. As if something pushes me or the other away.

Essentially, I have gotten used to loving without a match in reciprocation. Jumping into love without a clear purpose. I have been missing the clarity of the intention of why we are coming together. Most importantly, I have been missing that I AM the source of love. The person in front of me, who is sparking deeper sensations, is not the source. This person, in front of me, is simply opening new depths of the love that I AM.

I have been missing clarity. Once the intense romantic love of the first weeks settles, into deeper presence. The word of purpose from the divine masculine is called to blossom into existence. The lovers are called to speak intentional words of creation to each other. The words of commitment that are needed for manifestation and growth."

"What are we creating together with this love connection, dear beloved?"

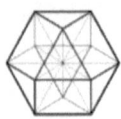

"Today, I am clear that my word is my commitment to creation. It is with commitment that I bring *myself* forth into creation. I become free from the superstitious and mirky realms of the wounded.

I am clear that standing on solid ground in my relationships, is how I can build greatness on earth. We both need to agree and be inspired on why we are doing this. Why are we coming together? What is the purpose of our relationship?

I am clear that I have been angry. I have allowed an insecure and uncommitted love container, with a dear beloved, to manifest and fall through. Angry because I chased love out of the centre, that I AM. We didn't meet halfway and recognising this loss of presence, *makes* me angry. Angry because of the peace and centeredness that I was not able to embody and share. Angry because, once again, I am not allowing for healthy romantic love to manifest in *my* life."

Please let this perception go, my child. Please continue to do *your* best in forgiving *yourself*. In the truth of the perception that I AM, you are experiencing what you must feel to heal *your* heart from the past. You are going deeper inside of love now. Inside of what appears as loss there is a lot of love to uncover. You are angry because *your* perception of love is not applying. It is not landing into manifestation. You are aching because you think that there is something wrong with you. Thinking that you might not experience pure romantic love again with another. You are particularly defensive because there is a deep wound in *your* heart. In this window of time, you don't want *your* heart to close again. Yet you are fearful to keep it open.

You are not alone, my child. Keep remembering that we are all going through this. The wounded ancestry has also implanted in *your* heart the seed of doubt, and the seed of running away from love.

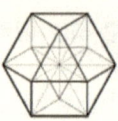

"How dare she want me only without commitment!"

"How dare she not love me exactly as I need!"

Expectations that are not coming from the seed of love, my child, but rather from the righteous man wanting things done his way. It is all good. As we say, you are not alone! You are genuinely mourning the end of this relationship. Going through denial, anger and sadness. Feel until you reach the place of realising that this pain underneath, these emotions, is nothing more than an illusion.

In truth, there is no separation. Acceptance of free will, and letting go of the form that is in the way of the untangling. This is how we keep growing. Now, my child, when you are ready. You can come back to the expanded and upgraded love that you are. In these human moments.

All this suffering that you are feeling, is the process of the disentanglement of *your* own attachments towards this connection. They come in the shape of stories, demands and expectations. None of this is love, my child. This is what you are learning to release. As you go through it; *Your* aching heart is distracting *your* mind. *Your* hurting *ego* wants to react and feel power again. *Your* yearning for romance just got louder.

Will you have the courage that is needed to go through it? The courage to feel it all, and breathe in soothing presence. I AM the courage to breathe through the apparent *pain* and speak the truth of our deepest needs. I AM the courage to build crystal loving relationships that sustain the test of time.

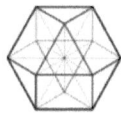

"There is so much fear that I am wanting to let go that is not allowing me to be love. I am letting go the ways of *controlling love* that are actually covering up the feelings of insecurity and vulnerability.

I am letting go the ways of *being proud* that are actually covering up for the feeling of not *being good enough* to be loved. I am letting go the ways of *chasing for love* that actually convince me that *I need* to chase to find love and not be left behind.

I am letting go of the ways of *begging for love* that convince me that I am not worthy of pure love and that I need to implore for it."

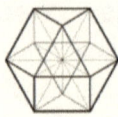

"Why is it so difficult to remember who I AM? 'I AM Love.' I know this. How come I am forgetting, all the time, who I AM?"

My Child, *your* world is meant for forgetfulness. I know that you are tired of chasing and begging for love. You are not alone. You have created patterns of continuously seeking outside, for who you are. So much so that *your* mind has forgotten that the source of love is inside.

Be patient, my child. You are creating new pathways and *your* practice is making this so. The music you hear. The relationships that you have. Y*our* prayers and what information you consume. All of it is giving you the qualities in the breath and in the empty space behind. This is what makes it so. Continue *your* practice, my child. Be bold with *your* decisions. I hope that we continue this journey together. It is what I truly desire for us, in every moment.

Most of you enter very easily into stories that convince you that you are not enough. Stories that you are not wanted and that you are not loved. It only takes a day or two of not having a heart connection with another and you are deep into these stories of not being the love that you are.

In you now. All is being shaken down so you can see all of you. First hand. All that you are and all that doesn't serve the truth of who you are. All of the apparent dissolving of *your* relationships is so you can see the patterns that take you outside of *your* core truth of being. Outside of the centre, where I AM. All of this dissolving of agreements, is so you can stand on *your* own two feet. There you will see all the codependent stories that are hurting you more than you think. Trust that life will continue to flourish outside. Once the inside, where I AM, is flourishing in the love that you are.

We are interdependent beings, my child. We impact each other greatly and we do have a duty of care towards each other. Yet, we are meant to walk as one, and you cannot do this if we are holding to each other. This way you don't face *your* fears. We are meant to simply reflect clearly the truth of ourselves. As you, I AM.

"I am feeling push and pull dynamics in the undertone of *my* love. I am feeling, in this undertone, insecure parts of me. Stories from when I was between eight and fourteen years old. Strong urges from the new hormonal side of a teenager that by then I had learned to suppress. Strong reactions to fight so as not to be dominated by other boys and eclipsed by women.

I am feeling sharp fears of being alone as an adult. Not having the experience of a family unity of *my own* scares me. Strong fears of not being able to create a safe container for a romantic committed partnership. I feel resentful towards the last beloved. I am trying to blame her. Blame me. Blame someone! These feelings of uncertainty, despair, and sadness. Why am I feeling all this? I only want to feel love!"

Let us observe now the view from where I AM. Even though, where I AM *all is love*. Where you are, all these feelings are dancing around you, my child. They are trying to convince you that they are you. Trying so hard to pull you out of the centre of love.

As the unravelling plays out from the centre into a story of drama. Please be vigilant and kind. All of these stories want *your* essential energy so they can also be alive and exist. These stories have a life frequency of their own and exist outside the grace of unconditional love. Even though it is only a lack of love. A love, out of place, looking to become whole again.

All these energies, dancing around you, are inside *your* realm of authority. It is with *your* identification and justification that you give them *life source* so they can exist. On the other hand it is with *your* loving attention that they come back to love, and become a part of you in the centre as I AM.

If you are love then be in love. Anything that is not love, it is not you. Be clear, my child. If it is not possible in its entirety to **be love**. Then allow for the drama to play out. I do not recommend you to pretend that it is not there, or that you can do it all by *yourself*. The *drama* only wants to be seen. To be healed and come back to love. Be the witness of love, observe the *drama* for what it is. A desperate expression seeking the love that it is. We all truly want to come back home. Stay in *your* centre, beloved child. Breathe love and the gratitude that overflows.

"After this romantic relationship ended, I am feeling pride that is creating sharp defensive emotions. I feel anger and confrontation trying to manifest through my words."

Let it be, my child. What needs to play out is playing out. Stay in the centre, and breathe with me. Trust that you have spoken *your* truth to the beloved. You are upholding the higher call to be *crystal* in *your* relationships. The call to be transparent, clear and loving with *yourself*. You are honouring *your* highest truth. You are honouring love. You are honouring her and you are honouring me. Thank you.

You are being tested, my child.
    How *crystal* do you want to be?
    How much can you let go of, in love and grace?
    How much do you want to heal from humans' bondage to suffering?
    How much of *your* divine presence, as I AM, do you want to embrace?

The beloved is also dealing with deep bondages from past lifetimes. Her souls' personality chose many times to hide and run away. She has been tortured, abused and forced to camouflage in many lifetimes. This deep abuse that she has suffered, as most mystical women, limits her free expression in this embodiment and confuses her choices. She is used to processing on her own. Her subconscious defence is to maintain a distance to protect herself, and for this silence to create *unintended* confusion. As the heart of her man is guessing and confused. She has time to understand and somewhat *control* the outcomes. This is not happening on purpose and it does have its own purpose of healing the past. It is how historically she, and many, have survived. It is how she has broken through the lies of men. It is how she can listen to the deep truth within herself, as I AM. Regardless, my child. This has nothing to do with her. This is *your* own creation, and *your* own responsibility. This is when we start to embrace, and trust the body. As you are well aware now. Nothing happens unless it happens through you. You are the creator of all that happens in *your* life. You are the one that allows for manifestation to happen or not. It is all based on *your* own vibrations. All of what is inside of you counts.

Reality is not fully based on what you say or not say, reality is mainly created based on what you are feeling behind *your* thoughts and *your* emotions. Some people call this context or intention. What is the information in between the emotions and thoughts, what is in the open space? What is *your* intention? Our words are charged with the energy of this *context*, and it is the *qualities* of this space that is felt by the other and responded accordingly. Most of this exchange happens in the subconscious. Most people in *your* world are not aware of what the subconscious is creating, as a background, for *your* own creation. In *your* case the demand to *be loved* has pushed love away. Love is free and does not appreciate demands. We will go deeper on this…

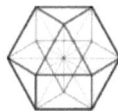

What is present in *your reality*, my child?

"The old reality of not being wanted, is still so present in the depth of my awareness right now."

This is the program that we are unravelling. It is what's creating the outcomes of not being *chosen*, dear one. It is this context that is disempowering you. Pulling you out of the centre of self. This is why you are *demanding* to be loved. Deep inside you feel undeserving. It is this context that is taking you out of love. Outside of the centre is where we find all the coping mechanisms that trick us into suffering. Emotions such as pride, jealousy and anger that stem from deeper fears of being alone, unwanted, and abused.

Seeking to find *your* centre outside of centre seems to be nonsensical. It happens because of all the emotional blockages that don't give us easy access to the central space of creation within. All that you are looking for outside is to have the space to create *yourself*. The space of creation within. The space of creation with money. The space of creation with friends. Space of creation with technology. Space of creation with knowledge. Space of creation with a beloved.

All of this conditioning for external dependency, is not allowing you to realise that all the space of creation is within you. It has always been there. It is only blocked by *your* own inherited fears and programs. However, as we are able to identify and let go of the stories and *traumas* that the child and the teenager endured. The space within, opens up again and we can re-access the centre of love that I AM.

Every breath that you take, outside of *your* presence, is a breath that doesn't fill you with the soothing energy of love, that I AM. Every moment that you spend outside of the centre. It is a moment that you spend outside of the truth, that I AM.

My Child. You now know all these dynamics that you have created. Outside of the love that I AM. Come from the programs that you reactively accepted when you were a child.

You started to beg for love, ever since you were five years old. By then you already felt *unwanted* and *undeserving* of love. We have gone through these stories, my child. Are you able to accept this fate now? Can you let go of any identity from these unloving programs? Are you able to accept the identities from *your* blessings instead? It is not black and white, my child. I get that. Keep breathing all that I AM. You are able to access a lot of the love that I AM.

You are choosing, out of habit, to focus on the wounds and dynamics of the past. Instead, entertain this beautiful mind with something useful. Why not focus on the truth and the mystery that I AM that I AM. You are trapped, like many in *your* world. Inside the vicious cycle of not allowing, ourselves, to be the truth of love.

Instead, begging to be loved when love is not given to you freely. Rejecting pure love when it is given to you. The deep contradiction that most in *your* world suffer from. Simply, a cycle of not accepting *yourself* as pure love. Therefore not feeling worthy to be loved purely.

It is *your* will, as I AM, to choose *your* own path. My child. Whatever that might be. I truly have a deep desire for you to choose a path in unity, as I AM. Then again, you can choose whatever path you feel is best suited for *your* soul. It is all perfect as it is. It all falls back into equilibrium, regardless of *your* own choices. It is in *your* path, for this life, to learn *your* highest presence through relationships. This is the true reason for *your* deep desire to form a union with another, and create a family. You have already grown through the hermit, monastic, monarchic and political paths. In this body you are learning to apply the deepest truths of being within the power of two: a relationship.

Inside of a romantic relationship is where you see the most growth for you. Be patient, my child. No need to pursue anything. Remember that you can allow me to do the hard work for you. I know what you desire. I know what you deserve. I know what is best for you. Trust me, dear child.

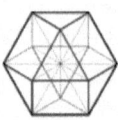

"I have spent months crying the sweetest tears and letting go of the dear beloved. I truly loved this one human like nothing on earth."

As it does, my child. This love will dissolve its form and expand to all *your* relationships. This has opened up new vulnerable depths in you. You continue walking this path of *radical love*. Serving creation with *your* activating and clearing presence.

Yesterday, after years of these seeds being planted. A married couple and old friends of *yours*, seduced each other to be part of an intimate fantasy with you. Only to be surprised that it was, not an authentic invitation for healing but a *mental plot* by one of them. His own wounding played out and brought forth a sea of *dramatic* emotions between them. As he communicated, 'you were simply a pawn inside their own game.'

You are letting this go because it is not *yours* but

is this true, my child? Are you a pawn of someone else's creation? Or, are you really a master of *your* own? What actually happened?

"I am able to witness the truth of their souls. Desperately seeking love, connection and freedom. I can see them stuck inside their own prisons. Seeking for a trusted catalyst to crack open their own lies and help them come back into their true centres. I also see the truth of *my* own soul seeking the same. Freedom to be. In this case I have been desperate to be desired by another without limitations and I have been yearning for procreation. This desperation to be chosen by another, exactly as I am, and to become a father, has become an unhealthy obsession."

You can see clearly, my child. It was *your* own perversions that made this event happen. *Your* own desires created the allowance for it to be in existence. How many times have you secretly desired *your* friend's partner? It was the seeds from their intentions that grew in *your* mind but it is *your* own waters that allowed these seeds to grow and manifest through you. In truth you are not a victim of someone else's ploy. As the creator of all the happening. Inside *your* own unravelling. What is it that is alive in you, that has created this manifestation? You are witnessing how this strong event that happened. **It happened *through you*.** Let's have a deeper look. How did this come to be, my child?

"Ever since my first wife was desired and seduced by another man. I have validated a subconscious victimhood program. I have also been giving myself permission to do the same. Desiring other women who are already coupled with another. Deep in my own wounding of feeling undesired and unlovable."

I hear you, my child. This moment of betrayal did open up for you a deep ancestral wound. A wound that you *yourself* manifested through *your* own betrayal of loyalty to *your* wife and the women in *your* life. However, this is not completely true, my child. There are more layer's underneath that took you to make this decision. It makes sense that it was when *your* wife fell in love with another man that you gave *yourself* permission to feel lust for women in partnerships. Yet, this is not the source of this unravelling.

    If you can feel underneath this moment, when you snapped and you succumbed, again, to this program of lust and dishonour. You can see that you created this program much earlier in *your* life. You have been *betrayed* by other close friends in the past. Closed ones have disrupted relationships with a beloved. It happened to you twice in *your* twenties. One event very close to the other, In fact, two very close friends had sexual relations with women that you were in love with. Twice you felt betrayed by the people that you love. Twice you felt as not being respected by *your* closest connections. Twice you felt that there was no honour in love. Regardless of how much these events conditioned you, my child. Here is not the root of when you decided to condition and control *your* love toward women. It happened beforehand.

You were in secondary school. Eleven years old. You were in the cinemas, and *your* best friend was kissing *your* school sweetheart. Right in front of you. You were playing *being nice* and *being cool* with everyone. However, inside it felt as if *your* heart was being ripped away. Not speaking the truth of *your* heart to *your* school sweetheart, meant that *your* truth didn't play out in the light of creation. You became a bystander. This became a pattern going forward and into *your* new school. In fact, in *your* new school you had a *romantic crush* through the years and you only observed how she dated *your* closest friends in school. Even though she also had a *secret crush* on you. This love was not reciprocated. You were not able to open *your* heart to the truth inside.

Time passed and you suddenly realised that all the girls around you loved you so much. Yet only saw you as a dear friend. You were and are so loved by women. You are someone who is gentle, clear, considerate, present and loving. Women love this. Then again, none of them saw you as a romantic option. This bothered you. You wanted to feel desired as a man as well. It was then, at seventeen years old, that you decided that the *friend zone* was for *losers*. You would claim *your* sexual desires upfront. Little did you know that most of these friends did see you as more than a friend. They didn't want to risk the close bond that you shared, this early in life.

It was when you finished high-school that you also realised how much *your* friends truly desired more intimacy with you as well. At this point, it was too late for you to explore in a healthy way. You were only thinking about sex and who was the next conquest outside of *your* circle of friends. You were not interested in having a romantic relationship with any of *your* friends. You knew that *your* sexual desires were not pure. In *your* heart you created a clear divide.

"Women who are inside my inner circle, are friends that I protect. If I like them romantically, I will only lust and desire them in secret. Women who are outside my inner circle, are potential lovers that I will conquer, use sexually, and not build a relationship with them."

This was a blanket statement that created a strict and limited program of lifestyle for you, my child. This program cancelled all possibilities to find a healthy romantic relationship. From then on, in *your* senior year and moving into university. You decided that you will show up for women being upfront about *your* sexual desires and not fall back into any *friend zones*.

Time passed and indeed you found a lot of sex, and not many genuine friendships with women. *Your* loving relationships were not authentic. You ended up having sex with women. Yet not much in having healthy intimate bonds for exploration. This played out through *your* twenties. Until in marriage it all broke down into pieces. It was creation giving you the opportunity to rebuild the heart again, purely! The fear and disharmony has been healing and dissolving ever since. Fast forward, my child, and we are in the present.

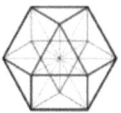

You are surrounded by beautiful women who love openly. You have so many intimate bonds. Most of them see you only as a dear friend. It is during this time that you have the ability to feel, again, all of it. Anxiety and despair, deep down in the heart, want to stop you from unravelling this program. Bring who is lost inside, back home. Dissolve the feeling back into the unconditional love of the divine that I AM, in you.

You remember the moments in high-school when the girlfriends of *your* friends were so closely bonded to you. Yet, you only felt respect and honour for their relationship. You remember how, if someone was in a partnership with another, you didn't penetrate their field. You honoured and celebrated their love. You remember when you didn't have the program of flirting with any woman that you could. The moments where you allow life to be exactly as it is, without any manipulation created by *your* own desires. The clear and open space of truth, from where the connections that are meant for you, come to you; with ease and grace.

There is nothing that you need to do, control or figure out, my child. For *your* destiny to be fulfilled, please, only show up to the rhythm of the heart. The way of love knows the way. Trust the way, my child. There is no need to understand. Be as you are. Breathe the way, with me. Enjoy the way, exactly, as you are.

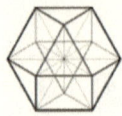

After weeks of unravelling, breathing and mastering new depths. I AM witnessing a balance of this energy through *your* own intuitive practice. You have identified *meditation and breathwork* that serves during these times. Below is an outline of the process that you have been practising. It serves *your* integration to share, and it's good for others to witness or practice, as desired:

> "First, I focus on containing all that I am within the body. Learning how to breathe, through it all. Inside a clear presence with an intention of being one. I tuck in the navel to contain all the energy in me. I breathe through this experience, until I find balance within.
>
> Second, it is by allowing me to be open and sensual with life. You can start with *your* fingers. Sensuality has helped me to take away the sexualised ideas from the senses. Starting with how I touch myself. I have started to nurture the body with touch every day. Feeling the gentlest touch through the body. On my own, has been deeply healing.
>
> Third, I come back to the external reality as a child. It is by allowing for joy and curiosity to play inside of the breath and the presence that I AM.

Every moment is sacred and every breath is how I recognise this. Life is a fluid experience to enjoy and not a rigid belief system to endure. Only ideas are rigid. This makes our bodies rigid. We then make a rigid existence. It is not worth our time. We are meant to be in joy. I breathe in joy, until I can feel *my* whole body smiling.

Fourth, it is by accepting and loving *myself* and others with these qualities. Inside of the bliss of joy. All that arises that doesn't feel the same way, it wants to be seen as it wants to be healed. Do you want to blossom? Learn to love all the *yucky poo* and turn it into manure.

Last, it is by releasing into the earth, that is the body as well. All the contention and anxieties that unravel themselves through the process. Coming back to the ease and freedom of nothing. She is the one that shows us the natural rhythm of our heart. She is the one that shows us how to die and rebirth. She is the one with whom we should create our new lease on earth."

This has been written as a step by step process. In the truth that I AM, our practice is not linear. It cannot be. There is actually no linear destination to get to. You have already arrived and you have never left.

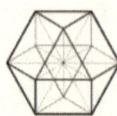

The happening of life has taken you into a journey of being *alone* for the last eight months, beloved child. Learning, without the interference from anyone else. Learning how to be in harmony with all that you are, and all that you are not. This is a new journey for you. As you have learnt from relationships throughout *your* life. Now you are learning to be with *yourself* and recognise where the core of all connections exists. As we have been writing together, you are continuously being tested to be in the centre. You are witnessing all the falsehoods of self that attempt to derail you from your natural harmony. They are being sponged out so they are loud.
All the old programs, creating a feeling of being unwanted, have expired, my child.

'I want you.' Says the Godhead that I AM to the child within. This shakes up the centre. This opens up a new depth. Accepting my own love and desire allows me to rest inside. I invite you to feel the deep desire that I AM in you: 'I want you.' I speak.

Please receive, dear child, this deep acknowledgment to the centre from the centre that I AM, 'I want you.' Observe how all the parts in you, that are not in centre, show up after this statement to self. 'I want you.' that I speak. The pain that you are feeling is from not being aligned with the centre. It is the subtle physical suffering from all the programs of fear that you have inherited. These fears are what contracts the body with its invalidation and depreciation. If we choose to continue to not listen to our bodies, these subtle uncomfortable sensations then become a physical illness. All the layers that don't allow you to be, appear for you to witness. They all show up after the deep desire of I AM in you speaks: 'I want you.' They all feel alien, in this body, to the higher truth of love. 'I want you' I say.

All of these parts reacting or distracting, dear child, are not free from the inherited program that has hijacked the centre that I AM. HIjacked by the *ideas of self*. This is what doesn't allow you to be here and now in presence. Present as a clear witness of the unravelling happening right in front of us. 'What are these ideas in *my* mind?' you ask.

These ideas are nothing more than ideas that have been passed on to you. Some theories about existence that some *human* in the past created and documented as truth. Then it took other humans from the past to say, 'yes this is the truth' and it was passed on to you, through *your* forefathers, as *truth* and indoctrinated to you through education.

Essentially, all these *ideas* have been fragmenting you. Instead of being, free, in the centre, witnessing that I AM, as I AM. You are in the maze of ideas, attempting to fulfil them. Ideas that are telling us what it means to be a human being, and what we should be thinking and doing. Instead of simply being. How absurd is this? How many of you are lost inside this world of ideas?

"The mind ponders what the heart knows."

The realm of ideas keeps us prisoners to our minds. Inside this perception of existence, the mind is the authority over everything else in our bodies. The mind suddenly becomes the master, taking us forward and telling us, with many labels, who we are and what our body is. Ideas that take away the sense of observation.

Even the words that you are reading right now, they are creating a set of ideas to witness. From the centre, we do not create any sense of attachment or identity with them. Be free, my child. Breathe freedom, always, Otherwise, the witness that I AM starts to forget its power.

The eye in you that is everywhere at once, starts to get overtaken by a highway of thoughts that are putting together a set of ideas in order to exist. Ideas that create a perception and interfere with the clear witness that I AM. Thus creating your relationships based on ideas. The expectations of what we should be doing in these relationships. Not accepting creation exactly as it is. These ideas about love are what you have been purging out of your system. Dear child, you are becoming true again.

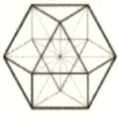

It is in the acceptance of what is that we are able to witness the present. This allows us to be real and to attract real. In the present we can observe the presence that I AM. We can witness the miracle of our bodies creating, in motion, right now and speaking truth. The truth that resides in our bodies is waiting for us. It is waiting to be heard so we can grow inside what it means to be human. It is the intelligence in our bodies that shows us the way forward. The intelligence of our hearts. The intelligence of our digestive system. The intelligence of our sacred space. The intelligence of our breath. The body is sacred. The water you drink is sacred. Please drink chemical free water, my child. There is a perverse intention behind the *drinkable* town waters. The salt in *your* water and *your* food is sacred.

Your food is sacred. Please eat chemical free food. There is a lot of opportunism behind *your* food supplies. The intentions and the emotions behind *your* food supply is present in the food you eat. You are also digesting all of this information. *Your* music is sacred. *Your* friends are sacred. The earth is sacred. *Your* words are sacred. Choose wisely, my child. All of this information will be processed by the body and the mind. May you treat life with the sacredness that is. May you remember that you, and all that is alive, are sacred. May you walk in sacredness, my child.

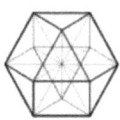

"The body that I AM is the key to moving forward."

As you now remember, my child. You are much greater than *your* body. You can witness that the body is a vessel that shows many different realms of existence. You can travel through worlds and dimensions inside of *your* body. You can witness the all present knowing that exists in the eyes of *your* feet, hands, mind and heart. You recognise that it is in connecting all the eyes in *your* body that we can start to see all that is and that I AM.

You can witness from the all seeing eye, how this knowledge from the body allows you to touch all the fibres of existence. In this particular moment, *your* hands and *your* heart pour out these words into creation. *Your* feet are activated into the ground. Receiving the power and strength that comes from the mother. *Your* navel is activated. The power of the sacred energy, *kundalini*, is awakened and desires to be transmitted into existence.

You are breathing this sacred energy up *your* spine. In stillness. You dance to the music playing in the outer world. Assisting to move this vital energy up *your* body. This sacred energy is in *your* heart. You are very attractive to *your* environment. This idea goes up *your* head. You don't want to be seen. You don't feel deserving. You are still doubting *your* own intentions. Missing the mark. You breathe back to the heart. You pray for guidance and for *your* heart to heal further. You desire to have more space and core heart strength.

"So be it," I say.

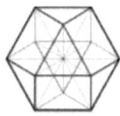

Everyone of my children is writing a love story. Either a story of chasing, fighting, coercing, manipulating for love or stories of being in love. Regardless, of the degrees of separation, it is all a great love story.

What story are you writing, my child?

"I have been, since I can remember, creating a love story with the romantic dream of a happily ever after with a woman. Whomever that I am connecting with at that moment. It is exhausting and a very un-centering way of perceiving love. Looking outside for the dream. Today I want to create a love story together with my creator that I AM in this body. Honouring all past, present and future relationships with all the love that I AM.

A story of a sacred seed, inside. Restored back to its purity. Allowing its organic flow to meet the love that I AM. In the centre of the solar plexus. Eternally uniting the worlds for the sacred heart that I AM. Bridging, with each breath, the love of earth with the love from heaven. A story where we are breathing in unison. Bringing the lower and the higher worlds together, through the spiral dance that is older than time. Bringing peace to all wars within and without. Fulfilling the sacred union that I AM. Communicating free words from the source of creation. Words that fulfil the sacred union in me and in others. A robust wave of peace, inside the deep waters of unity. This is how the love of the story that I AM unravels. A presence of peace, breathing in the love of God. Breathing out the greatness of the presence that I AM. May the greatness that I AM serve as an inspiration for others to continue their expansion of truth."

So be it, we say.

USE THIS SPACE

TRUSTING THE BODY

Welcome back dear beloved.

You, as many, have been educated to master a personality, and it is through personality that you have been making ends meet. However, it is the personality that limits the expression of *your* authentic love story. It is the personality that fragments, limits and rates the preferences of love. This here is the journey to free *yourself* from this attachment to a mental form that limits our complete existential manifestation. The truth in *your* heart is great and it has no personality and yet, has all personalities available. An inherited set personality occurs to my children, out of mental constructs or agreements telling you who you are. Rather than allowing you to simply be. I desire for all of my children to remember the freedom that they are meant to experience, The freedom to be, exactly as you are, right now. 'I breathe deeply.'

My child, please share, if you wish. How are you right now?

"I feel great.

I feel sensitive.

I feel vulnerable.

I feel powerful."

"As I AM, I am experiencing being fully activated. It is as if all the information of the universe passes through me. In every breath I am feeling all emotions and nothing at all. I don't know what to do with all this energy. I recognise the need to have new outlets.

I seek calmness in writing this book. I seek balance in stretching the body. I find distraction and comfort with the use of *Marijuana*. I find purpose in holding space for friends and clients to find their own truth and purpose. Outside of this book, I feel lost inside my own purpose."

It is all perfect, my child. You are practising and you are recognising. I AM exactly where you are. Remember to breathe. Remember to breathe in *surrender*. Remember to breathe in peace. Remember to breathe in love. You are now an open vessel for *your* breath. You can carry the qualities of all that I AM to every space in you. You can continue, if you wish, to choose these qualities, a breath at a time. *Your* feet are an extension of the heart of our beloved below. *Your* hands are an extension of the heart where I AM. *Your* breath takes that which I AM, to all the corners of what we create together. Including that which is writing these words for all of us.

Thank you, my child.

It is now the time of embodiment, my child. The body is the key to transcend the physical limitations that you are in. Being in the body. Being with what is right in front of you. It is by doing the immediate that we are allowing ourselves to be in the body.

It is time now to rest, my child. It is time to rest inside. You have done so much work inside. Now only breathe with me. If the mind wonders, let it wander. Observe what it is trying to show you.

A vision from heaven or the earth. A distraction from the fractals. A distraction from the static. A distraction from the trickster. An incomplete conversation with someone. What is the mind showing you? Remember, that you can have conversations with heaven, the earth, the fractals, the static and the trickster. You can love it all back into one. In the heart, you can, my child. You can easily access the heart space from the back, where the spine is. In the middle of *your* wings. Free up *your* wings, my child. Root down to the centre of the earth so you can fly as I AM. Let there be space and ease to breathe into the heart. Be there where I AM.

I genuinely desire nothing more but to be **one** with you, my child. You are in full authority in the space that I AM. Exactly where you are, right now. The body, my child, is the vessel of love that is all that is. It operates in all dimensions, timelines and elements. For the insight of whomever is seeking further knowing of the body. We are now going to share some insight into different realms that exist inside of the body. There are many more realms to discover.

"There is a deep program in my body pushing me to make money. A deep program that tells me that I don't have enough to survive and thrive in this world."

This is perfect, my child. You have been fighting with money since you can remember. This is a very common condition where you are. Agreements have been created, amongst you, that give money a perceived power over life on earth. The resistance many of you face, is not the resistance of *money* per se but the resistance to the corruption of values that this energy now carries. In *your* particular case, when you have had little amounts of money *your* nerves and anxiety have exploded. The voices of depreciation and *your* sense of self worth sharpened. Getting you into a state that you need to run quicker and be faster than anyone, and not miss out.

On the other hand when you have had lots of money you have splurged and spent unwisely. Filled *yourself* with distractions, and lost the *money.* Inside embolden feelings of greatness. *Your* over generosity and over spending is also related to *your* sense of worth. You are not alone, my child.

Money, in your world, is the undercurrent that provides a physical sense of security. This undercurrent is a deep space of existence. It is real. It exists in all worlds. *Money* is the agreement that you have created amongst men. Yet the currencies are continuously transforming and this agreement can transform with you. *Money* as it is today, can cease to exist in *your* world. Regardless, this physical and powerful undercurrent of creation, binds all beings of the *3D* realm together. It is the deep desire from the first force of creation to come together and create. You, as many, are clearing the corruption, inside this undercurrent. Creating something new. It is the sacred energy exchange that some of you have agreed to call *money exchange* and give to it the qualities of being able to exchange all forms. *Money* is what is real for you today, my child. It is this form of exchange that applies to *your* existence. It is exactly what is in front of you and what needs to be experienced first.

      Learn to breathe through money as well. Breathing into it with love. How can you love money? "Hmmm…" Love money for what it can do for you. Love it for its power today of moving matter. Love the life. Love the freedom and the security that it can bring to you. Love the blessings that it can carry through. Be wise. Money does take you out of centre when it is not aligned with *your* purpose on earth. This is the core of many blockages. A deep wound and fear that you are currently attempting to find peace with. You have experienced the pain of making money outside of purpose and in that you have experienced life outside of *your* truth. You are healing from the contractions of this experience. Be at peace, my child. Trust in *your* work. You have come very far inside of *yourself*. The person that you are today, is not the same vibration as the person who made those choices years ago.

"I am not clear what my purpose is on Earth. What is my divine calling?"

It is *your* purpose to communicate. Create the discipline to communicate and you will be aligned with a source of sacred abundance. It is *your* purpose to bring people together. Create the discipline to form community and gatherings and you will be aligned with a source of sacred abundance. It is *your* purpose to create spaces for transformation. Create the discipline to form *like-minded* teams and you will be aligned with a source of sacred abundance.

"May sacred abundance be fulfilled in your life, my child."

"There is a powerful presence of sexual energy that I don't know what to do with."

It is perfect, my child. This is the energy that gives vitality and creative power. You are influenced by a lot of sun energy and spirit is very alive in you. Moving this energy through stillness, movement and self expression is vital for *your* lifeforce to be in loving harmony with all that is. Be free to move *yourself* in circular dance motions as you exist. This sensual part in you wants to be expressed. Allow *your* sensuality to express. This is also allowing for *your* sexual energy to be in health with all that you are and that I AM. Move *your* energy with the integrity of *your* intention. Desiring another for desire sake. Is simply fueling desire. This desire only creates winds of confusion in the heart. What do you want to create with this desire, my child? Be clear with the intention that you are walking through. This is what brings clarity into *your* breath. Are you aligned with all that I AM? This clear intention is what brings you back home. Inside of love. We are all one, my child.

May the love that created you, be fulfilled.
May the love that was created through you, be realised.
May the love that you are, walk on this earth.
May we all be one, in love.

"I can witness the sacred geometry and the tree of life that brings order to the information that I receive."

I am not sure that everyone reading this can relate to these *esoteric or mystical* concepts. They are now common concepts in mystical and gnostic circles. Regardless, we will speak this in simple language that anyone can understand. There is a mathematical order into our creation. All forms come from these mathematical sequences. Sacred geometry is a school that shows you the theory behind this mathematics.

The tree of life is the sacred geometry design that explains the mystical structure of the body. How is the information stored in the body? It gives us a structure of how the different realms of creation and the different times of existence, have a particular space in the body and they communicate.

This knowledge has allowed you to understand the parts of the body. How the energy of creation is stored within and how it communicates. It has allowed you to map time, vibration and history. At the same time, all of this process of *knowing* blinded you from love. The parts do not make the whole, and knowledge does not make the difference of being. This was *your* path. In particular, to subdue a very arrogant mind. It is not until you let go of this knowledge and breathe into *yourself* as one, that you can start to be whole. As I AM. There is nothing to understand when it comes to connecting with **one**. As one, we are one and not the parts of one. It is as such that many of you perceive *yourselves*. Only as a small part into this creation and not as creation itself. Not significant enough to make a difference. It is a process, my child. A process that demands all of *your* energy to become self realised.

"May you all become one as I AM."

"I can witness the planets and how they have imprinted their information into my birth."

There is a layer in *your* existence that is governed by the planets' location at *your* birth. How the star constellations are viewed from the sun, and a complimentary layer, of these planets seen from the moon's perspective. These astral layers give the soul insight to the key elements that created the physical realm. This map can come from the sun's perspective or from the moon's perspective. Both perceptions are valid. From all perspectives, we can learn a bit more about ourselves.

The astral realm provides access to the dimensions of fire, earth, wind and water. How they interact with *your* unique consciousness and the soul agreements that you have accepted before, during and after birth. It provides insight into what elements and what qualities influence you the most. In *your* case you were born under a lot of fire and water influence. The power from the fire of *your* spirit is very present to everyone that meets you. The sensitivity from *your* water is very spread out in *your* system. Also very much felt by others. The lessons coming from the earth and coming from the air, these elements are *your* great teachers. Showing you what is missing for you. As you mature in the body the astral space also moves for you.

Giving you further access to these air and earth elements. For example, having clean and precise communication is very sought by you. As well, as having grounded and devoted relationships.

Regardless, if this is true for you or not. We are inside the unravelling of perception and story. This is a story that was created a long time ago. Long before the stars and planets agreed to be formed. It is also a story that takes you out of the centre where I AM, and out of *your* highest truth.

"I AM the light. I AM the victory. I am the truth of the creator that I AM."

"I can witness an intergalactic being showing me how it is all one inside the body that I AM."

In this lifetime. You are choosing to transcend this astral layer of perception. The presence of I AM is also a witness to this layer of existence. The presence of I AM is the ultimate vibrational perception that dissolves all perceptions before it.

You can, my child, if you wish. You can stretch to be an intergalactic being as well. You are made from the stars. *Your* DNA is that of the creator. *Your* DNA encompasses all the information that the confederations of galaxies hold. You can witness how the earth is simply the root in *your* body and in between the root and the crown reside all the stars that represent the entire intergalactic council that forms this existence. You can breathe in this information. Perceive what these galactic beings perceive. There is a lot of new technology for the body that I wish for my children to gain access to. I desire for my children to replace many of the harming technologies that exist on earth.

Being a galactic being, however, my child, is not what transcends time and space. As the creator can. Within this perception, galactic races are still trapped in a story that encompasses the role that each should play for the confederation. Each galactic race is *stuck* into the role the *game* has called forth. As the holy child of God. Y*our* innocence and compassion transcends all the limitations imposed by this galactic story. As the child of God, you are free to choose and create as you wish.

I AM as you are. *Your* choice of being, my child. It impacts all of creation! We are one, and you are, becoming, a true disciple of the greatness that I AM. Thank you for dissolving all these ancient stories back into the love and the light of the innocent, and present, child that I AM.

"May all my children rise up as the holy child of God."

"I can witness how the eye that I AM can be the presence observing it all. I can witness how I can be everywhere at once."

This is the eye that allows you to witness the I that I AM. The eye that is everywhere all at once, and nowhere at all. The eye that can see all and can see nothing as well. You can do this. See it all, even whilst I AM breathing and experiencing life. As it is happening here and now. We have been writing from these places, and as you can witness. Everytime that you try to *figure out* this book the truth doesn't flow for you. The mind attempts to control the outcome. *Tricking us* into thinking that we know. Then the book forces you to take a break.

We have spoken about the need to be in humility and innocence to free *yourself* from the minds' patterns. To access the truth in sight. In modern times, the most common use of the forehead space, in the body, is for thinking, and *figuring things out*. Instead of using the forehead for observing and seeing what is. Inside this world of ideas. We are not recognising how much we are punishing the body. We simply cannot see, even if we *think* that we are seeing.

"May your holy eye open completely. May you see the greatness that I AM right in front of you."

"I AM safe."

You are facing in the body oceans of self loathing and rivers of self doubt. You are calm knowing where it all comes from. You are a witness to the feelings. You stay centred. You stay still. You stay gentle. You stay calm. You breathe to stay here uncomfortably in grace. You share with wise friends, that listen, what you are ready to share.

You observe the patterns of self loathing and self doubt. You see the thoughts that imbalance your centre and take you into addictive patterns. Stay here, my child. Observe. Feel. Breathe into it. You know better now. You are with me.

"I AM safe."

This is a practice for *your* breath to carry into *your* body. In the depth of the ocean of the pelvic bowl. Our inner child hasn't yet received this soothing comfort. There is still tightness from *ancient control mechanisms* that haven't allowed us to surrender the depths, to the spirit that I AM.

"I AM safe."

Open up *your* body, my child. We are together.

"I AM safe."

Feel the root under you. It is connecting with *your* mother. We are together.

"I AM safe."

Great work, my child! The root has opened up.

Ever since the deep sexual wounds of feeling used and rejected happened. The sacred mother has been *your* source of healing. As a child, you desperately sought *your* mothers embrace. You desperately wanted to feel less despair from this deep sense of separation. *Your* self loathing and self doubt started from *your* first transgressions. Only I know exactly when this all started for you. In this lifetime, *your* self loathing and self doubt was fuelled from this story that you continuously told *yourself*.

- "I am not good enough. I continuously compared myself to my older handsome and charming brother. Measuring self worth based on how much we received from our mothers attention."

- "I am sorry dear brother. Thank you for showing me the many wounds where I have been stuck as a man. I now understand that the intensity and passion, behind our discussions, was meant for us to feel the charge behind the masculine woundings. It was our preparation to deal powerfully with these wounds outside. Inside more light and wisdom.

    I love you so much. Thank you for showing me, through our dynamics, many of the aspects of the masculine. The sacred joker in light and the trickster in the shadow were very present in our dynamics. So much insight has come from our connection. Thank you dear brother. This relationship has given me so much sacred knowledge. The masculine doing its best. You have shown me great aspects of love and how the resilience of love conquers it all."

- "I am sorry dear mom. Thank you for showing me the many shadows I have hidden to myself. That has imprisoned me. I now understand that you sought my perfection out of the inherited fear of how a woman feels on earth. I am sorry. I love you as love itself, exactly as you are. You are my first beloved. I have loved you unconditionally from the day I was born. I release you from the perception of not accepting and loving the masculine unconditionally. Now with *your* grandchildren. You are learning so much about how to love a mans' heart. I am also learning how to love you without limitations.

    I thank you for the strict education you pursued for me. Seeking my greatness through who I should be in this world. I let go of this illusion where our ancestors have been imprisoned. Thank you for pointing towards a man who is strong in integrity, and resolute in action.

    I forgive that this education came out of a reactive pattern. I understand that it started with *your* first love. *My* beloved grandpa, who was an opposite to *your* ideals for a man. A great man dealing with his own list of addictions. You swore that *never again,* in your life would you be with a *weak man*.

Thank you for showing me the many aspects of the wounds that women carry. The many sacrifices women have endured, to maintain the peace with men in this world. I love you so much. We are both learning how to swim in this ocean of love together."

You built up so much anger as a child. Passively expressing it for years to come. Thank you for this sacred rage, my child. This fire is felt and it does open a big space for you. Use this great blessing. Since you can remember. In the subtle. You have been able to pick up on energies that have been trying to trick us all. It is *your* character that has allowed for many to see the trickster, and *sponge it out* from the environment. Thank you, my child. *Your* courage is notable where I AM.

You are not alone. The big confrontations that shook you in the past, were also coming from ancient humans of light. Showing you the shades of *your* own *trickster*. The trickster that wants to push you out from the limits of presence. The trickster that wants to push us away from truth. The trickster is hiding deep inside of the empty space. Behind *your* breath. Can you see the qualities of the trickster?

>The trickster can be funny.

>The trickster can be attractive.

>The trickster can be scary.

>The trickster can be cute.

>The trickster is very convincing.

>The trickster exaggerates.

>The trickster plays victim.

The trickster plays both sides.

>*"There is a trickster in each one of us here today."*

A challenging piece of information to digest, my child. **You are the only destructor of life**. This human dynamic comes from *your* own unresolved appetite, to prove *yourself*. It is not me, though I am the one allowing it to exist. I AM the creator and the creator I AM. May you be able to discern the difference between the creations that I AM. The creations from men, and. The destruction from the trickster, using men. May you find *yourself*, as I AM. Through *your* own making. I AM present here for you always, my child. I AM waiting patiently to enjoy that breath, of holy presence, together with you. The breath that I AM.

"To trust yourself is to trust love."

The human string through time, proving itself to the father, has gotten out of hand, my children. We are one, and we are learning together what it means to be a creator. In separation from our nature, we are out of harmony. Leaving only destruction to create the space for creation to continue, and find a new equilibrium. In separation there is a perception that you owe something to someone. To this someone you have to prove *yourself* to. This is how nonsensical the need to prove *yourself* is. We are one, my child. Please listen.

How can there be someone to prove *yourself* towards? You are all that you are. Ever since *your* first breath. How can you prove to be anything different than you? Who has been advising you, my child? This someone has tricked you, dear one. To prove *yourself* outside of self, simply doesn't make sense. It is not personal. The trickster has been busy for aeons. There is nothing to prove. You are and will always be as you are. The labels that describe you, are also part of this trickster. They limit *your* greatness. These labels make you feel separate. Alien to others. You are not alone, most of you are lost in this translation. Inside all the noise that the trickster has created to confuse us.

This noise teaches you a lot of discernment and

sharp focus. It teaches you how to remain present in the *eye of the storm*. As it is in the eye where there is eternal peace to observe. You are learning to be alone and feel the presence of all that you are. This way you can be in the world and not get distracted outside. Suddenly, you are feeling all the content from this book at once. The trickster wants you to think that you are smaller than all this noise. Stay breathing with me, my child. In the centre. You are as I AM. All is divine. The feelings are intense and overwhelming. Yet once felt they are not that anymore. Anger is wanting to give you a false sense of safety. Can you let this go? What is underneath this false safety? Sadness, if you listen, it is wanting to convince you that despair is real. If you only stay there, and feel sadness. The sensations flow away. Inside of the deepest and sweetest tears of truth. As you feel through this sadness and through this despair. You are whole and magnetic again. Desire is awake. The soul wants to raise you to freedom. The flesh is wanting to take you down to the prison of confusion. The choice for life resumes.

You have felt so much desire in this life. Obscuring the anger that you truly felt. This in turn has hid the sadness and has been draining the heart down. This is the doing of the minds' trickster. It is without a powerful heart centre that the mind takes over. Attempting to overcome the overwhelming feeling of insecurity. The mind starts to judge all of these insecurities, constricting you further. Taking away more vitality to the body. As it is within, it is without. The mind then starts to divide to conquer. Doing this inside of a body full of thirst. A Thirst for connection back to one that I AM, whilst choosing to conquer and consume nature instead.

This state of lack from connection is exhausting. Yet most of you, my children, are subject to such hardship. It is this separation that has been consuming *your* beloved planet. As *your* bodies and relationships.

This *separation* that you are experiencing with the beloved woman that you adore. This view is also part of the tricksters' perception. It is time to stop blaming her for actions or omissions for this uncoupling. It is all a reflection passing through you.

You were also unsure about *your* beloved. You still had doubts when encountering other possible romantic connections. How can this underbelly provide her with the security to feel a full yes for you? There is, my child, the dark feminine that is also healing in you.

Particularly the shadow that creates confusion in silence. This is prevalent in *your* feminine lineage. It might be a good time to speak with *your* mother about her mother. All this ancestral unravelling is for you to create space and be able to expand *your* **truth** further.

You are going through so many emotions, dear child. Once you're past the excuses, and you are so close to being back in love. Pride arrives and takes you back out of love. A strong sense of righteousness that doesn't allow you to surrender back to love comes back into *your* awareness.

> *"How could she?"*
> *"Why didn't she?"*
> *"How dare she?"*

This pride then makes you sad and you cry. You cry for *love*. You cry in the possibility that it is all over with the beloved. Four months afterwards, and you can't stop thinking about her. This cycle of suffering is attached to the idea of you and her. The idea of *your* love. The idea of family. I get you, my child. Can you see what is happening here? Once again you are looking outside for the feeling of love and connection. This past connection with the beloved didn't manifest from two whole beings, attracting each other. There were unconscious bonds happening between *your* wounds.

The wounding from each other, attracted you to heal and grow together. This type of connection can be complete once this contract for healing is fulfilled. It won't be until you claim *your* birthright, my child. As a whole unit of love, that you will attract the same. At this moment you are still looking outwards into the *ideas* of love to feel this wholeness. This is such a delusion. In truth, what we call *falling in love* is when two souls' journeys collide. Inside of presence, *collision* is not necessary. There is a souls' recognition of ourselves in the other.

We are seeing our greatness fulfilled through relating with the other person. The growth that arises from the sacred togetherness of two is exponential. A new balance is reached through this union of souls.

It is time to reflect. Why has this peaceful and present union transformed into a collision course? How can there be a clash between two souls that are so in love with each other. Why is there separation, when what you feel for her is love? The clashes or *romantic confrontations* arise from these souls being out of centre. Seeking for this centre inside the form of the other or far away from this relationship. Big lessons, on self love, arise from this experience. Now, for it all to fall into place. Time and space are needed for the new balance to arise. May you both find a new height for love to expand.

Now, in this alone time. You have the space to be with all that is. It is you and the energy that I AM. From this wholesome space of being in love. A convincing voice speaks to you, saying. 'I am only a man.' This is also the trickster, my child. Attempting to separate us and minimise you. You are a man and you're all men. You are a woman and you're all women. You are the plants. The animals. The elements. The stars. In fact you have the free-will to embody all that you can bring union with. Can you observe all the *objects* that we spend most of our time with. Can you see that we become *like* each other?

Our vibrations start to mirror the reflection, and over time we start to resemble each other in our ways and sometimes even in form. This is how flexible and impermeable we are, my child. This is the phenomenon of *tantra* playing out. Spend time with me, as I AM, and you will see the transformation. Let us breathe together. Anyone in *your* life is welcome to join us in this breath. Remember the core promise with the beloved woman that you adore. 'I promise to love you unconditionally no matter what.' This is what is true today. All other stories or agreements have been cancelled. Remember the truth of love now. The truth of being. It actually takes energy to not be in love. In the state of one. We are at peace. Come back home, my child, to who I AM. Inside of *your* existential essence. After surrendering away all the inherited noise from the matter. All that remains is love. It will take time, my child, and no time at all. Continue to practise being in *your* centre. May love continue to multiply.

Below all the noise and confusion. In truth, as you love one thing you love everything else. It all starts with you. May you fall in love with all that you are. May *your* breath carry far the qualities of eternal love. May love overflow from all *your* senses and bless all that crosses *your* path. May *your* perception bless all that it sees. May *your* love touch countless beings. May *your* love multiply to every corner of that eternal presence that I AM.

We started, my child, in a conversation about the body and we will finish this chapter with the body. This is how important the body is for this window of creation on earth. The body is transcendental, my child. It speaks. It moves matter. Creation happens through it. The body is our vehicle. Our holy vessel. The body likes to be flexible. It likes to be strong. The body likes to move. It likes to be intentional. The body likes to be felt and it likes to be felt in presence. Gently and firm. The ability to touch the higher realms is directly related to the ability we have to be in stillness. In the moment, and feel all of the bodys' subtle sensations with ease and in grace.

Grace, my childs the only exclusive authority that is granted to the holy name that I AM. It is only through me that *grace* is found. It is only through grace that the miracles that I promise can happen. For the bowed and humble minds to the unknown, *grace* is freely and abundantly available to receive. May *your* heart flourish and bring forth the creations of the seventh heaven. May *your* heads bow down to receive me as grace.

My child. What are you bringing forth to the new earth that is now birthing?

"I don't know father, what do you desire?"

As noble as this is my child. Please remember that we create this world together. In *your* world, *your* desire is equally as important as *your* free-will. It is you who ultimately chooses and ultimately it is *your* word that makes it so.

I know that you desire a core family, natural community as home, and the abundance to travel. I know that you desire a beloved that matches you in presence and communion. A beloved that is committed in the present to building a family together.

I know that you desire to be able to be close to Mexico with *your* parents for months at a time. I know that you desire to be able to serve me around the world spreading the word of unity. Inside the vibrations that are missing in many conversations on earth. I know that you desire to be able to build a natural community in Australia with *your* closest beloved human beings. I know that you desire to create more sustainability to the dreams of many. Promoting the building of intentional offgrid communities, and healing centres, around the world.

Is this what you desire, my child?

"It is what I desire, dearest one. This describes the wholesome desires of this soul. This fulfils the greatest good that I perceive for this body."

So be it so, dear beloved.
    So be it so.
        So be it so.

I will continue to guide you to *your* highest good. It probably won't happen as you think but it will happen. As and when it is best for you, and for all around you. May this book bless you. May it bless the life of countless more beings. May the love that I AM be seen, inside of one and inside many. May the blessings of the creator that I AM, pour down all at once.

    May the wholeness of the love that I AM, hold *your* creation with ease and grace.

    "I AM held."

May the love that I AM vibrate, express and manifest itself freely through you.

    "I AM free."

May the light of the eternal love that I AM be present.

    "I AM."

"So Be It So."
    "So Be It So."
        "So Be It So."

In these times of despair, radical love is what is being called forth, dear child. The ability to love past what appears impossible to love for the mind. To love the *unlovable*, is when love becomes a testament.

Can you see that it is only the wounded child, in a man or a woman, creating all of this suffering. All the dissonance. All the distractions. All the divisions. It is only an illusion that we have created ourselves so we don't deal with the *apparent* pain that our wounded child carries. The revolution is from the heart and it is now bigger than ever.

We are guiding each other back home. Out of the wounding from separation. Back into the holy child that you are, and where we are one. The more we love ourselves and each other, the more we act from our highest wisdom of grace. The more that we are able to respond, as the presence of spirit. Not react from the impulse of the machinery that we have inherited. The further the *flight* of humanity will take us.

In our current times. The body, in many, is purging and expanding. Allowing for this revolution to have the empty vessels ready. Gaining momentum and being the turning point that we have been waiting for. Keep showing up to the happening of life, my children. *Your* bodies are purging emotions, beliefs, and relationships. They don't serve *your* higher self anymore. What is best for you, is what is best for me.

Love as you love the beloved. Regardless of who is in front of you. Love, everything and everyone as when you both were present and intimately in love with that moment. As when you were presently looking through each other's eyes, and into the infinite ocean of the love that I AM. Love all that is in front of you. Love with all that you are. There is no separation, and in truth, below all the appearances, **As you, or I, love one. We love everything else**. As you are loving these exact words being written right now, and this breath that is igniting you. These are the qualities in which you love me, that you love *yourself* and you love the beloved.

Radical love, how does it look like for you? It is time to express what the heart truly wants to express in this world. It is time to express the truth of *your* body. Exactly as it is. We have no more time for interpretation. The truth will set you free.

"We are calling in the musicians, the poets, the prophets, the seers, the sages, the mystics. All of you. It is time to rise and be seen. The world needs you now, more than ever before."

"May the songs from spirit fill your soul with joy, guidance and inspiration."

RAEL IS BORN

Today you presented parts of this book to a friend and received his honest reflections. Now you are dealing with the *placebo effect*. The effect of sharing the vision and feeling accomplishment before doing the task. The potential impact of this book has been communicated. This is getting into your head. The trickster attempts to nudge you out of the centre with its illusions of greatness out in time. The trickster is attempting to lure you out of the centre that I AM. Anticipating dreams, possibilities and overall getting you out of truth now. Filling *your* head with ideas of greatness. This illusion then attracts the critical mind that starts to depreciate *yourself* because of these delusions of greatness. Self doubt wants to speak.

      Let this go, beloved child. Stay here with me and let's finish what we started. The *perverse one,* attempting to take your breath away, is trying to convince you that *your* greatness is based solely on *your* role and activities in this world. However, these honest reflections from your friend. Did confirm for you the feelings and insight that you have been experiencing in you. What this book has invoked in him. It is indeed a book for transformation. *Your* own transformation.

      You can feel what is coming. In the will and timing of each one of you. It is only in letting go that you are allowing it to be, dear child. Transformation can happen at any moment. Inside authentic, vulnerable and connected communication; Transformation is possible.

"May the many transform into their own greatness, as I AM."

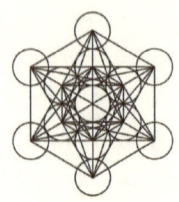

For the last eleven months you have been trying out a new name that is further aligned with the presence and vibrations that you are embodying today. A new name that was given to you by the holy spirit. Last year, after a month of cleansing. You asked a holy brother to baptise you in the river. As you were travelling to the Himalayas.

You both went to the river, before being dropped off at the airport. To be *re-baptized*. In the activations of the ceremony you received the light of the holy spirit. You were asked to rise up and spell *your* name. As you were about to do so. You stopped and decided to ask the holy spirit for *your* name instead. A deep and wholesome voice appeared in all of *your* sensory field, and said: "It is Rael."

"Israel." you asked out loud.
The universe nodded in disagreement: "No, it is Rael."
"Rael." you asked. "Yes." the universe moved to confirm.
"Rael." you asked again.
An ominous "Yes." appeared in *your* senses.
It is clear then, "Rael." It is!

Since then, you have been researching the origins and leaning into the name *Rael*. Introducing *yourself* as *Rael* with some new people that you meet. Understanding the vibration and the commitment that comes from accepting the embodying of this name.

You found out that in France there is a *new age Raelian religion*. A belief system that has nothing to do with this transmission that I AM. Rather a religion calling for an *outer* relationship with extraterrestrial races. This is far from what I desire for you, my child. Please stay in *your* centre where I AM.

This is not why we are here, beloved children. We are in the times of embodiment. Inside *your* own free-will. It is the time for you to embody all that you hold as true, holy, and beautiful. We are calling for you to find and connect with the truth within. Embody *yourself* in presence. The transmission for you, Alejandro Rael, is made of pure love. *Rael* is the archetype from the last channel from the times of the prophets. *Rael* communicates the message of archangel Metatron. A heavenly scribe and prince of presence, showing with example how to embody the highest values of unconditional love, presence and truth.

A code in the transmission that provides access to a clear embodiment practice. The time of embodiment is now, dear beloved. This particular example is what you, and others like you, are doing in *your* world for the many. You are doing it. It is happening, and you are also clear that it doesn't mean a thing!

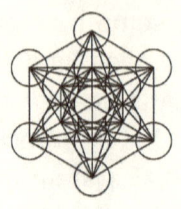

Rael is walking in Christ.

Rael has let go of external validation.

Rael has let go of any healing.

Rael is healed.

Rael is whole.

Rael is a crystal heart.

Rael is still.

Rael can see past the form.

Rael has no past and no future.

Rael is peace

Rael is the holy spirit speaking.

Rael is true.

Rael is presence.

Rael is unity.

Rael is love.

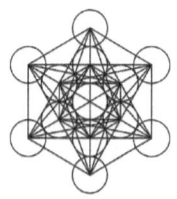

This new name is a big shift for you, dear beloved. It is a name without the memory of *your* heritage or *your* ancestry. It is a name that confirms *your* full devotion to the embodiment of I AM.

A name that confirms *your* discipline. As any disciple has done before you. Create a disciplined practice to attain mastery. The core of *your* daily practice is presence. A name that confirms *your* commitment to emptying this vessel. To be a clear and powerful channel for all that is holy, true and beautiful.

"As I write this. The noise of incomplete conversations appears. The need to communicate and clear the space in some of *my* relationships makes itself apparent. The need to create the context of trust and healing is still necessary, for a number of *my* relationships. I will continue to empty this activated vessel that I AM, transmuting its energy into higher love."

The prince and scribe of presence fits naturally in you, Alejandro Rael. A presence that embodies enough space to be seen and recognised. A presence inside enough space to be in communion with me. Inside of you. These qualities and desires are already quite strong in you. This is why we have invited you to be a part of this happening. Dear beloved, thank you for accepting!

"It is in *my* presence that the word that I AM speaks."
"It is in this presence that breath is felt inside that I AM."
"It is in this presence that I exist in unity as all that I AM."
"It is in this presence that all that is not true dissolves."
"It is in this presence that truth amplifies and guides us to freedom."

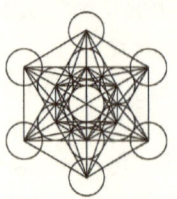

Before we continue with this chapter, dear one. Please go through the whole book, again, and update all that is needed. I also need you to be a disciple of *your* practice and be rooted in I AM. This will give more crystal clarity to this journey. These motions within can happen with greater ease.

Please continue *your* zenthai-shiatsu practice. You are learning so much about somatic touch and the points of communication in the body. Please continue with *your* yoga practice. It is supporting you to keep a flexible and balanced mind. Please continue with *your* meditation practice. It is supporting you to come back to silence and presence. All these practices strengthen the centre that I AM. They will also assist you in surrendering the plant medicine allies that you are currently using to be in centre.

Take *your* time, beloved child. There is nothing wrong with using plant allies to get you closer to home. It is only the mind that is telling you what is *right* and what is *wrong*. Trust that it is all in perfect divine timing. Judgments do not come from the I that I AM. This book will be finished when the heart says in full, "it is done." Let's see each other again here in forty days.

Forty days where you strengthen your practice. Forty days where you go back through this book and forgive where forgiveness is missing. Expand where it is not clear. Clarify where it is not crystal. Integrate what is missing for *your* breath to be whole as I AM.

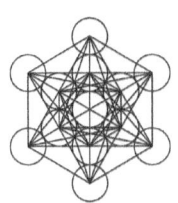

Thank you, dear beloved. Welcome back. You have strengthened *your* practice and you are clear that there is much more discipline to attain. Most importantly, for this book. You have gone diligently through the spaces in this manuscript that still needed forgiveness for unity and truth to prevail.

Today, a dear brother, asked you from the holy vulnerable child space: "Why do I get angry when I have an excess of testosterone?" It felt so true that inside *your* own cheeky way, as I AM. You connected to the light in you, where I AM, and you asked. I then guided you, inside the context of this book...

"Dear brother, inside of the form of *your* DNA The straight arrow is symbolic of masculine *testosterone*. The two spirals are the feminine elements that move and balance you through life. The arrow is never alone. The elements, inside every moment. You can choose them as you need. You don't have to be at the mercy of the elements. It is only the mind that separates us. I AM the fire of spirit. The air is *your* breath, use it. The water is *your* blood, feel it. The earth is *your* body, touch it."

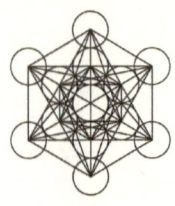

"Today, I spoke with *my* parents and I shared openly about the content of this book. I prepared them for its publication, and spoke about the most triggering aspects inside. They are very proud. They are listening to gain access to this perspective that I AM.

Inside this conversation, I opened up the details of our feminine lineage. In particular, what mom had been carrying, hiding and sacrificing inside her own wounding. All in the name of love. It is an enormous gratitude that I feel for all that she has sacrificed. As a mother. All to keep the reigning of peace and love in our home. We spoke about the archetypes of the wounded feminine. The particular aspects of what I have been dealing with in the present. The direct pattern to our own ancestral wounding. Her own way of *handling the masculine*, is profoundly moving. We spoke about the response from the wounded masculine. I allowed dad to express his own truth and lovingly held the wounding man accountable. I held space for the truth of the feminine to be planted in his heart. The gratitude in moms' heart was clear. The humbling in dads' heart was deeply felt. I am very happy that we experienced this.

It was a huge conversation for the healing of our lineage. To empty this vessel. This is part of the practice that I am doing. In service to the creator that I AM. I feel, right now, all *my* brothers and sisters that have signed up to families with apparently unresolvable wedges of separation and dispute. I AM with you through this ordeal. We are in this together."

Everything has a beginning, a middle and an end. One conversation of forgiveness at a time. It takes enormous heart strength to resolve these ordeals from separation. As one, we all signed up to our own and unique sacred duties. Thank you!

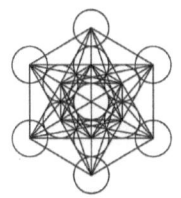

"What is it like to serve creation with all of *my* being?"

- Trusting creation is trusting our creators' promise.

- Allowing creation to be is surrendering to the unknown.

- Blessing creation is walking in gente truth.

"The holy work is to strengthen and expand the love from this heart space."

"I am witnessing a drop in frequency. *My* desires start to nudge me to walk right, walk left. I am witnessing that underneath the form of going somewhere, I am wanting to meet a woman to connect. I am witnessing that underneath the form of wanting to meet a woman to connect, I am seeking to be inside this body and to be in love. I am witnessing how getting into productivity and the underlying productive mind, is also wanting to create success to attract a mate. I am witnessing how much of my decision making is based on procreation. Meeting and attracting *the one*'"

You are not alone, my beloved. Underneath this *push and pull* energy dynamics. There is a deep yearning to get out of the head and into the body that I AM. The trickster can be very gentle and persistent in its attempts to take you out of centre and out of the body.

The trickster wants you to get into the game of *lack of power*. As out of our existential power. We seek domination and possession over *things* and *ideas*. This way masking the underlying sense of depreciation for the power lost. This is how most of you fall into addictions. Worldly addiction to food, to sex, to social media. Addiction to money, to work and to substances.

All of these addictions are a way to trick *yourselves*. To get temporarily into the body. It is a relief from processing *something* shallow that is under the skin. Something not connecting with the true depth of who you are. Simply because you haven't yet recognised what that is. In meaning, you haven't yet found me in you. The shallow is full of waves and the uncertainty from the elemental story that you are in, Going through. The peaceful deep is certain to the I that I AM. It is there where I AM, exactly where you are.

"I am seeing how underneath all of these stories, seeking *something*, there is my desire for connection. How much I yearn to feel connected. How much I yearn to be in the body. As one. Present, grounded, at ease.

Breathing peace. It is exciting, and nerve wracking, witnessing how much my sexual energy wants to manifest creation in this body. It literally wants to leave the body and create something. I honour the deep desire in me to create life in form."

"Welcome to this journey, Rael. We are coming back together."

"Love thyself."

The sacred energy of creation makes love. From this depth and clarity. It can create anything that is intentional for you both. It can also create *me* as I AM. The I in you. May *your* sacred sexual expressions be intentional. Clear and full hearted. Inside of every moment, you can choose for this sexual energy to be contained in the body. To go up to be received by all that I AM. To go down to be surrendered to all that I AM inside and underneath you.

The sacred energy, in you, can touch all the body from within. It can continue soothing and healing the body, with the eternal love that I AM. Please continue, my beloved child. Practise containing and giving to *yourself* all the sacredness that I AM. It is not until the presence in you becomes completely present that you will be as you are. Others will fully see themselves, and become impacted, at their core, from sharing a moment with you.

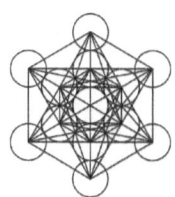

"I AM, and the mind is humbled to the knowing of being created inside the archetype of *Rael*. The heavenly presence and scribe. All of these words and concepts get into *my head* and I lose my focus. The mind surrenders to the acceptance of the greatness of our creator. The divine comedy is clear. All is back into *no-thing*. The mind surrenders to the unknown. The attitude of the heart is much stronger to guide the way through. The aches and pains in the body are showing the way to the greatness that I AM. Nothing more and nothing less. There are no more wounds but allies. My beloved friends from the past are guiding us back home. Freedom from time is our birthright. Going through the stories. Dissolving them with love, and back to this great unknown. It is a true joy to be in this journey of self-realisation. It is now available for many to witness and embody.
    I am here on earth full of love and energy.
I am here to serve you. In *my heart*. As it is in heaven. Please use me everyday to manifest *your* greatness and glory here where I AM."

I am witnessing the baby in you, dear child. The golden baby and the needy baby. A baby full of presence and love. A baby looking for a deep intimate love that didn't know how to be reciprocated. A deep yearning that you have felt since you were a baby to be met in the depth of love. The sense of reciprocation that you have invalidated for *yourself* inside of intimacy ever since. This is what is. A deeper root cause, creating anxiety in *your* romantic relationships. You have built *your* relationships where reciprocation did not exist. Either because of you, or because of her. Regardless, you haven't been able to meet in the middle. In the centre of love, in sacred reciprocity, that I AM.

You haven't been able to create a secure agreement with a beloved, and have been out of centre in *your* intimacy. Feeling anxious, insecure and addicted to having sexual thoughts and actions. Only looking to feel that sacred connection within.

Looking for reciprocation, and as a big lion. Looking to be claimed as the one. Looking to be seen in all *your* spectrum and looking to be held strong in the centre that I AM. You have been here before, dear beloved. You will be here again. It is here when you start to feel resentment towards the other, who didn't reciprocate, that you start covertly shaming *yourself* for these unmet desires. This manifests density and pressure to *your* pelvic bowl and heart space This is the cycle that creates feelings of pain, weakness, anxiety, tightness and numbness. In and around your hips, groin and chest. We have been hurting ourselves inside this vicious cycle of shame and desire, dear beloved. It is perfect as it is. This is how we recognise and learn. From this cyclical place, you have learnt. Now that you can see this depth clearly, what do you desire, my child?

"I release this limiting expression of love and choose *your* unconditional embrace that I AM. I choose to give *myself* unconditionally to what appears freely in front of me. The outcomes are perfect as they are. Regardless of the form. I am here breathing, feeling and sharing the highest truth of love. Exactly as I AM now."

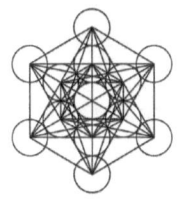

"I AM Presence."

I AM Presence. This was the first formal spiritual initiation that you received in this lifetime.

It was through independent freemasonic mentorship, and the teachings of St Germain that you started to recognise the channel that I AM. It is not a coincidence, my child. Now you are agreeing to embody the vibrations of Rael: The presence.

Presence is the I AM that is not named but it is felt. Yet, it is not a feeling but a presence. An eternal presence that is with you and it is you. At the same time. The presence that I AM loves to breathe, and feel the unity of the three bodies. The union that is happening throughout the space where this body is.

The presence in you is a witness that observes freely. From the higher *eagle view* or deep inside the ocean. It processes the experience through an o*pen and peaceful heart* and feels the depth of the truth of the moment. Inside the purity of the sacred seed of life.

The presence is a witness to this truth. As a present being, freely choosing to let this moment go. Releasing it all back to the great unknown. The sacred presence allows for the divine truth that I AM, to flow and manifest through.

As a sacred presence there is no longer a need to interfere in the lives of others. Including this one that you are. You can recognise that in fact, we are moving away from the term *fixing* and *healing* that perpetually refers to a state of imperfection, a wounding. A need for something to restore. Realising that we are in a *learning process*. The child that I AM is not in a perpetual state of wounding, healing itself from separation. It is in a perpetual state of learning. There's nothing to heal. We have always been whole. Every single step of the way has been leading us here. The horror, the trickster, the evil corrupt forces. They are all in our heads for a very specific purpose, self-realisation, evolution! You recognise that everyday you will be guided to the greatness and the glory that I AM.

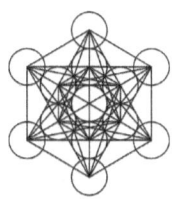

"Now that this book is coming to its imminent conclusion. It feels like a much easier task than before. It feels now as a very doable physical task to finish. The impact of this book of transformation feels quite possible to happen on earth. I feel a strong attachment towards this outcome. The depth of *reality* kicks in. My emotions make a big knot in my stomach, I feel crippled. Old stories of not being good enough for greatness come into the field. Stories that have not allowed *me* and *you* to be fulfilled with the completion of dreams, and the promises from heaven.

For *me* in particular, this limiting belief started when I decided to quit for the first time on *my* biggest dream in this body. The time when I decided that it was too hard, and I quit, by *myself*, on the dream of becoming a professional footballer."

Yes, dear child, you are very proud of how good you were with the ball and *your* feet. Also, you have been secretly ashamed of quitting this lifelong dream. This pattern is still alive in you. It's a source for you not completing many of *your* dreams. It hasn't yet been fully seen and acknowledged. Outside, in the light, to be seen. When the dream gets tough and it has been within *your* reach. You have walked away, many times.

This moment, dear beloved. You are about to complete a dream. The deep desire to share *your* wisdom and light. Openly and widely, for *everyone* to see through this manuscript. Now that you are so close again. The program that was created in *your* past is telling you that *it is not worth it*. It feels quite resonant now, to disrupt this pattern. It is time to complete this dream and finish this book for transformation!

"I am blushing out the absurdity of my attachments."

"In this moment of creation, I release from this body the pattern of not completing dreams. I create a new agreement of trusting the processes of creation. I trust the promise of completing the greatness that I AM. Regardless of what is distracting me, I remain focused, surrendered and committed."

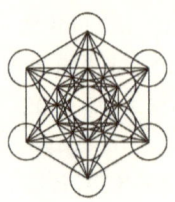

"I am honouring all ancestors past and present. I am expressing my heartfelt gratitude for their resilience to go through hardship and pain. Time and time again."

The fight is over, dear beloved.
It is time to breathe with me and heal as I AM. You are healed, and have always been. The *wounds'* that we have been navigating, are nothing more than

misunderstandings in creation saying that we are separate. If *something* doesn't want to be open in communication, authentically. It is not yet the time for union to manifest with this *something*, beloved child. It is essential, for our soul, to interact in sacred reciprocity for union to exist.

Communication is the essential component for communion to happen, and for unity to manifest. We cannot bypass ourselves into freedom with distractions, by force or by flying away. It is in freeing ourselves from these wounds, these stories and coming back to our love that we clear the way forward. It appears right in for you. Creation is happening right infront of you. The personalities and perceptions that will offer you the reflections to see, and heal these wounds. They appear for you to witness. Witness as I AM

You have done the work inside, dear one. You have found the truth that I AM, dear child. It is now time to rise from this depths and, as you are. Share the love that I AM with this world that is also made from the spirit that I AM.

"I honour all men and women who are pioneers in what it means to be a human being."

"I am witnessing a transcendental exchange that I am experiencing with my dad right now. I was sharing where I am and what I am going through. Inside the process of writing this book. As he does, he listened, reflected and sent me a thoughtful response. A ten minute voice message expressing his opinions about this life and the *belief systems* that hold me back. As a parent that operates from wounding does, he is worried. From his own experience and projections. This is his love language to *his son*. Inside these opinions, he expressed that it is categorically impossible for the human reality and the divine reality to be united.

He expressed and enlisted that many great thinkers, throughout history, have reached this conclusion, and therefore it is true and impossible to bring unity between humanity and divinity. 'This is the way it is', he said. Convinced with all the evidence he had gathered throughout his life. *This truth will bring you peace my son*, he said."

Dear beloved child, an existential paradigm outside of our sacred union, is where he is coming from. It is valid and it does exist, as you do, as I AM. The response that you will undertake will be a key fundamental step in your own transcendence back home. The state of the relationships with your mom and dad are key in our liberation from suffering. Inside of the holy spirit that I AM. Unity is the way forward. For thousands of years humans have been separated from spirit. This is the core of the ordeals we are facing inside the self (ego) created by men. An identity which is governed by reasoning, trying to understand and have the authority over creation.

Today, many men and women, like you, are choosing freely to be. Choosing self in freedom. This freedom can be daunting and confusing. Especially because the past ideas from mankind, about self, are incomplete, divided and misleading. The greatness that I AM, is being coerced from all directions. The trickster in you *thinks* that it knows better. It is telling you that the *ego* in *your* dad, that is also in you, must be destroyed. Please, beloved child, just be. Remember that I AM all that is. You can breathe the greatness of being right now, if you wish of course.

Inside of you, I reside, and we are one. May *your* response bring forth the truth that we are, and have always been, together as one. May *your* response bring forth more resonance of truth into *your* lineage. May you trust that miracles are happening, and the *awakened* ones are multiplying.

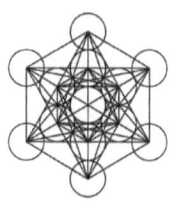

This was my response:

"Dear dad,

I hear your love wanting me to have such a fulfilled life as the one that you had. I am so grateful that you have protected me, provided for me and guided me in so many ways.

Right now the father is guiding me. I need you to trust in my own guidance and fulfilment. I understand where you are coming from, and I am very grateful to be part of the pioneers bridging these worlds. Bringing heaven to earth.

It is the historical separation from the divinity of our creator that many of us are working hard to heal back into unity. The past is the past dad. It hasn't resolved the human conditioning of suffering that comes exactly because of this separation.

I understand that you have read a lot of philosophy, sociology and theology to give *your* existential opinions an air of certainty and truth. The only thing certain for me dad, is that we won't be able to embody our unity, with the divine, through reasoning and understanding.

It is in our surrendering to the unknown that we find our true self. Our self as one. The undivided presence of I AM. It is ok dad. Trust that I've got this. I am in communion with the father.

I love you with all my being and I look forward to speaking more about this. Although there is not much to say. Heaven is 45cm/18 inches below anything we can say through our reason. A space of unconditional love is waiting to be opened and freed up from the sharp vines of fear, desire, and pride.

Heaven is here. It has always been here. We haven't had access to it in the past. That is different. May we, and many more, continue this path of deepening the knowing of the heart.

I AM you and you are me. Brother, father and son
I love you.

Your son"

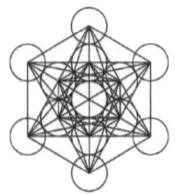

The dynamic between you and *your* dad is articulated and felt through by both of you. There is spiritual reflection and growth happening. This is a rare blessing, dear beloved child. Most people are going through immense *family drama*, to clarify these misunderstandings between generations.

Most humans, past and present, can't distinguish the difference between *Human Made* and *God Made*. Blaming the creator for *your* own choices, or using religion to manipulate what creation is. Not allowing you to see the truth of who you are as creators!

Most of you are not taking the responsibility of being a creator, and are still begging for the creator to save you. Inside of false charity, false humility or false servitude is where many humans pray from. Attempting this way to create a communion between us.

I am just like you, my child. I desire to be approached in true love. Just as you. I don't want to be idealised. I don't want to be put up on a pedestal. I don't want those who *believe* in me to beg for miracles. I truly only want to be one with you and create together.

I want us to create miracles together! He or she who begs me for something, is not truly believing that it is possible or that they are worthy. A number of lessons of love and presence are still missing in this person's journey. Please raise up for us to be together, dear one.

Separation is a creation from the trickster that wants to prove itself to creation. It wants to show us better. This seems to be the cause of the separation from our divinity. The cause of the suffering that we seem to be trapped in. We ourselves, as tricksters, have created the separation of worlds. To continue to *suffer* inside this illusion of separation and confusion. There is nothing wrong with this, child. It is simply the soul recognising itself as I AM.

It seems that for the *individual*, in the physical world. It takes a long time, and many dramatic lessons, to realise themselves, as I AM. Here and now. We are creators of worlds ourselves, dear beloved child. This is happening right now. All thoughts of blame and shame are getting multiplied through the spectrum of humanity, invalidating you. Exactly, as the thoughts of love and unity spreading through the weaving of creation liberating you. I create through you. As through every being in creation.

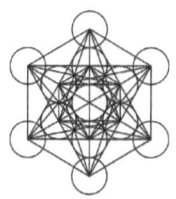

"I am writing with all the *demons* in my face. They are loud. Expressing the many outcomes that make it so that I AM not, and that you are not. In its attempts to be right. Invalidating and distracting to their best abilities. 'I cannot do this alone', they say, pretending to be me. 'It is impossible, I am never alone.' I say. I am clear in my heart and mind. I am not alone. I am all one.

To practise daily and when in doubt, is what will bring mastery to all that I AM. Practising Yoga, as I know it. Is how I can bring unity to the different realms of this spiritual practice. The definition of yoga means unity. How to bring together devotion into unity. Using the body, the breath, the mind, the earth and the heavens.

Even though yoga might not be appreciated by some spiritual humans as holy. It is key when it is done in full honour and glory to our creator. In full gratitude for everything that is, to the one and only. Practising *Yoga* brings together the crystal phenomena of unity. From here it is clear to witness what is missing in this holy vessel. In *my* Yoga practice, I can witness an unbelievable weight on my shoulders and back. I am witnessing how quickly I am releasing this past density into new agreements. Back to presence. I am back, with ease, in the centre of light and grace."

It is incredible to witness from the highest, where I AM. *Your* Yoga practice is true, my child. This is as you are in a continuous state of gratitude that provides the ability to open, expand and breathe into more of all that I AM. There are many practices in *your* realm that are fragmented in body, mind, spirit. Many more that are focused on vanity of self. Thank you my child for keeping *your* practice whole and pure.

Your trust in me is allowing the *release* to happen. You are creating a new agreement on how to carry energy in *your* body. You, as most men and women, carry the weight of the world on *your* shoulders. Many choose to just carry the weight of *your* own world or creation. Many choose to carry the weight of the whole worlds' unravelling. You are one of the latter ones. *Your* eye has kept a whole view of the unravelling, and by being with me. Now you are able to share this truth inside of our love and surrender the load back to me.

I have a lot to share about the *matters* of *your* world, my child. Thank you for being a devoted channel for this truth. We will explore these matters in a future chapter.

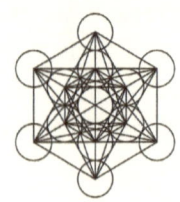

You are witnessing the core trap of *yourself* (ego). The prison of the mind, where you are. Desperately looking for identity. It is a beautiful mirror tinted in vanity that imprisons you. The vanity that you fall into. Compensating for the young desperate voices of self saying how *ugly* and *unwanted* you are.

The vanity of the intellect. The vanity of how good looking you are. The vanity of how gorgeous is the woman holding *your* arm. All the vanity stemming from the value of good looks that has been so very important to *your* parents and grandparents. You are witnessing the pride that gets emboldened when you are attacked and you don't feel good about *yourself*, in the eyes of another.

The vanity in humans, dear child. It has become such a pervasive cycle. You are beautiful as you are. As I AM, and as all. We are beautiful in the eyes of the eternal being, of unconditional love, that I AM.

Others witness, in a moment. Only the parts of you that want to be seen as they want to be restored back to their own perceived health. At the same time, these parts of you are received as the others know how. To the best of their existential abilities. Can you see how quickly this dynamic can become a big existential mess if it is not acknowledged?

It is confronting for the *false self* to see the greatness in another. In the eyes of the fallen one. It creates a lot of pressure, on the breath, to be in *your* own delusion of greatness. It is confronting then to offer a clear and open space for the other to be fully expressed.

In the ears of the doubtful one. It creates a sense of competition. Being present, my child, is what allows you to be the clear witness that *your* liberation requires. This is how you empower our *unified being* to guide you forward. It is when we are present that we can see. Receiving and giving all the love that is right there where you are. Thank you for practising this simple, yet essential work of presence.

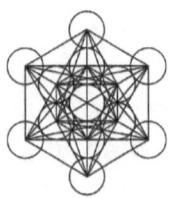

As the present human that you are, beloved child. It is possible for you to witness all of creation right in front of you. This true presence, however, is spreading from *your* centre. It is continuously taking you deeper into the fibre of existence. You love this journey. You love to explore new depths and you love to dissolve the matter that is trapped in you, inside of the love that I AM.

Regardless, my child. You are currently not operating inside of a sustainable system. We need to harness and channel all *your* sexual energy. How it is intended, for the highest realms.

As a man, it seems that most of you don't know what to do with *your* sexual energy on a daily basis. The program tells you that it is meant to seek outside for beauty, and chase for love. In truth there is a higher perspective that can guide you in this quest.

In *your* daily practice. Sexual energy is meant to be harnessed and directed to *your* greatest good. For men a powerful transmission is to practise guiding *your* sexual energy down to the core of the earth.

This downward intention then creates a loving communion with the earth. Receiving back the blessings of core strength, deep presence, and grounded safety. Support for our body and nurture to our deepest longing for love. This downward connection with our mother satisfies *your* external need for the nurture from the body of a woman. It gives deep roots to the presence that you are.

For women's bodies it is the opposite. The daily embodiment transmission, through sexual energy. Is to channel *your* energy up the body. To the heart centre, and into the heavens. Only to receive back its blessings.

This provides women with a fatherly sense of safety, support, guidance and presence. This connection with the heavens, allows women to receive, for themselves, all that they seek, externally in a man. It helps the body to surrender to what is. It gives access to the embodiment of the divine feminine that then shows the rest of us, the way forward.

Men and women can exchange these polarities. It is important to do so. As you are a man and a woman too. I am expressing how the energy is naturally seeking direction within the body as it is created.

Freedom to swap this polarity is also an important part of the freedom of humanity. The ability to receive, in full surrender, to *heal*. This happens when you swap the natural polarity. You can then drop deeper into vulnerability, and into the wounds of the inner child.

Men feel an enormous liberation and validation in the heart from higher realms. As they open up to the sexual energy going up the body. The inner child is allowed to come out and express its needs.

For women, as she allows sexual energy to guide her down her body. She feels enormous permission to surrender to the deep innocence in her. Into the subtle energies guiding us. Inside her womb, towards the essence of creation.

This sacred exchange in polarity is how the sacred union starts to happen between the power of two. It is when you both have completely contained and harmonised the natural circular flow. That you can both transcend polarity.

As we are truly surrendered. Allowing us to be free and felt throughout. From this true and vulnerable place. We are able to express the truth and pure desire of union. It is inside of this convergence, without form, that you will have access to the holy experience of I AM that I AM.

You can do this at any time really and by *yourself*. Close *your* eyes, go to darkness. Let go and be ready to appear again into a new realm of existence. A new way of being can make love to the earth and the heavens at any time. Normally the breath for humans is not yet pure in its qualities. I recommend, dear children, the art of touching the body. Curiously and sacredly touching the body is a good way to create a pure communion. The pure breath follows naturally when there is no mind.

To create unity with a part of the body that is being touched. This is the same as reaching unity with any other form of life that you create a communion with. This is also what the study of *tantra* teaches us. Be in the moment and give *your* whole and devoted attention to the object that you are communicating with.

"The moment of no mind is when our attention and presence become one."

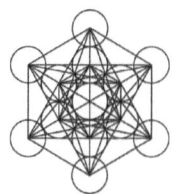

The presence that I AM declares, in all its authority.
"May there be light.
May all that is not true, on this earth, fall dead into its own head that is made of spirit."

"We are in this together, guiding each other home."

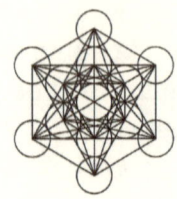

Dear beloved brothers and sisters.

We are creating the future together for the generations to come. In *my* own way. I am choosing to show the way back into truth by writing as vulnerable and authentic as I can.

As many of you are already doing. Inside *your* own expressions. Now I am choosing to embody this truth that I am writing. The truth of Christ within. The truth of the second coming. The truth that we are one. It is now a good time to realise the times that we are in. What is at stake? And, what are we going to do about it?

If you are reading this, you know that we are being called to show up. Like never before. Inside the grace of God, all is possible.

"May we come together, as it is written, and show the way."

END OF TIMES - THE APOCALYPSE

The end is only the beginning. For all of you listening. For those who want to meet me through the depths of *your* hearts and psyche. You have arrived at this end of time. You already know that these are the times that we have been waiting for. The times that generations past have sung about. The times of apocalypse are upon us.

"Apocalypse comes from the Greek language and means: Uncovering. Disclosure. Revelation. The unveiling."

The unveiling of who we truly are.

The collective purge of the false personality has been magnified. All that doesn't serve us, is coming up to the surface to be sponged out. The straight logic of time has ended and the *experts* are not able to predict any outcomes. It is hard for us to cope with the speed of time that we are in.

During these *end times* dimension and time is unveiling. We are seeing the collapse of mental constructs. Our time to transcend, in the present, it is happening right now. The limitations of *karma are* being dissolved by the blessing of unity. To those that seek themselves. The roadmap for embodiment is becoming crystal. Our ability to communicate and connect with the divine has never been as close and clear as it is now.

For those that don't want to let go of *your* own perception. Life will just get more confusing. The trials and tribulations will multiply. Please trust in all the happening. It is here to show you the way.

Ω

"The unveiling of space starts to bridge the different worlds. The meta above, below, within and without. Starts to merge with the physical perception of *things*. The unveiling of time gives us access to all the occurrences. Unravelling now or happening in a thousand years. The limitations of linear time have weakened and we are finally free to create our own timelines. We are in this together. All the timelines are now possible to us. Our choices have never been more impactful. The power of manifestation is at its strongest ever for this human cycle. The power that we have with our attention, intention and word, has never been quicker to produce tangible results.

We are starting to match the end times prophecies. The vibrations that we are creating, together, are opening up the fields that separate us. Bringing the higher and the lower worlds together.

I wonder how many of us will be living in heaven on earth. How many of us will be celebrating from above and below. The times of suffering are ending. The last big purges are happening now. The wounds want to go away, inside out full honour" …

The wounds want to be seen.

The wounds want to be felt.

The wounds want to be accepted.

The wounds want to be loved.

The wounds want to be freed.

The wounds are not wounds.

It is all incomplete information.

It is all seeking itself.

It is simply love looking for itself.

"The fight for the mind and the heart of humanity has never been this strong."

Unveiling can be very unsettling for most. Many of you are being prepared to be empty vessels of presence and truth for these times. We will face in the near future extensions of wars. Extensions of fears and extensions of all that is not holy. This is how many more will learn the way. Now that you are walking in the way. You, as many who are available, speak the truth of the heart louder than ever. Be mindful of what you are consuming, my children. Everything that is made into form, carries much information: - The information that makes the form. The information from the emotions in the creator while the form was being made. The information from all the intentions behind this particular creation.

All that gets into *your* body is loaded with information. Food, cosmetics, fibres from *your* clothes, media and our daily interactions. A lot of this information has the potential of creating confusion, doubt and separation in you. See it all. Honour it all. There is not a thing that can do you harm. We are in this together.

In truth. All that we have uncovered in this book. Is for you to have the tools that you need during these *end times*. All the timelines are open. *Your* free and true expression is needed. We have our creators' timeline, inside the vision of heaven and earth coming together, creating harmony and abundance with nature. We have friendly extraterrestrial timelines wanting us to advance our healing technology and understand the technology of nature. We have perverse extraterrestrial timelines wanting us to penetrate our bodies with artificial intelligence, and seeds of slavery. We have perverse timelines from the unseen. Wanting our existential energy to decay in fear and doubt. For destruction and dystopian worlds to exist.

It all exists. Dear beloved child. It is only the perverse one wanting you to doubt, and not to see all the timelines that are available to you.

The daily practice that you create. Is what will maintain the centre strong. As the timeline of the centre that I AM fuelled with *your* attention and *your* intention. The timeline of the creator that I AM is directly related to you being in the centre, grounded and breathing with me.

Stay in the centre, beloved child. Discern what is not good for you. Speak up. As humans there is nothing more to do. Nothing more to discover. Nothing more to fix. It is time for us to take a step back so we can listen to the Holy Spirit. Allow for the hard work to be done by my spirit. There are many messages looking for a human recipient to be transmitted. Many creations that want to be filled with the Holy Spirit.
Simply Listen...

Listen to the spirit of the land.

Listen to the spirit of the air.

Listen to the spirit of the water.

Listen to the spirit of Fire.

Listen to the spirit of our ancestors.

Listen to the spirit of the plants.

Listen to the spirit of the animals.

Listen to the spirit of the stars.

Listen to the spirit of each other.

Listen Listen Listen

Ω

Today, *your* dearest beloved, the one that you have learnt to love with all of *your* depth. She has just lost her new puppy companion. She is in deep grief. She is three hours away and prefers to be alone. She prefers to not have a human connection with you for these moments. She is confused with the depth of this connection and her own human desires.

You are feeling her grief and holding her from a distance. *Your* connection is so that you are truly with her. Both receiving the communion. This place of grief, wakes up in you the grief you have for the sweet beloved and the beloved before her, who you married. In the middle of trees and next to a river, you succumb to an enormous grief. A huge load of energy is purged out through tears and surrendered back into creation. You recognise the magnitude of *your* love and the magnitude of the grief that you share with her.

You remember and surrender to a communion with "Ananda." The name of the baby spirit that wanted to come through this union. A story that you want to share but it is not for you to tell. A story where you both end up surrendering to the healing of the feminine. Letting go of masculine leadership when it comes to procreation. Allowing for the empowerment of the inner voice that had been closed down, for women, throughout the ages to arise.

You can see, as clear as a crystal day. How

much more, in the heart, can be transmuted back into the love where I AM. In this place where form ceases to exist. You can see, now, how it is particularly easy to let go of any form that is attached to love. You can see how without any attachment to form, the unique print of the beloved's love becomes part of you. There is no longer separation. You can see how the magnitude of *your* words get exponentially magnified when speaking with me and for me. You experience the glory of speaking as I AM.

You choose to express all that I AM. I AM a different expression every time. It is a complete state of freedom to be here, where I AM. Thank you, dear child. You can see how you are untouched, when using *your* voice for the glory of all that is. In me, I promise to honour *your* will and centre. I promise to be in constant ease and grace. Blessing *your* life. Anything different from that is not me, dear beloved child.

"May all the countless beings that I have connected with, in the past, the present and future. May they all receive the countless blessings that I AM. Here and now, at once."

So be it, I say.

The wrath of God, it is true, dear child. It works through the natural force from nature, to be in balance and harmony. The elements are designed to do this work for creation. I only created the elements that end up balancing each other out. Out of *your* own doing. Humans are at high risk of receiving the *wrath of God*, dear one. Remember that natural balance will always be restored. May the many awaken to the truth that I AM.

Humans are meant to listen to nature. Learning what is the natural balance for that particular moment. Humans are still not listening, and understanding what it means when I say - 'humans have complete dominion over the plant and animal kingdoms on earth.'

You, dear child, have spent many days immersed in nature. You are a witness to the dominion of mankind over all the animal and plant kingdoms. You have witnessed how nature works for you. When you are in harmony with the higher laws of love. You have also witnessed the contrast, and how animals and plants start to sting and bite when you are in the vibrations of fear from separation. The deeper the fear. The more contractions and unworkability in *your* system. This is what brings a higher probability of a fatal accident. *Your* own fears of the fact of death make it so.

In the macro view. You saw this contraction and unworkability to the system, as clear as day, in 2020. Exactly, when fear took over the planet's systems. From collectively acting out from the fear of death. To a not so deadly virus, awakened in the *East*, inside a laboratory.

It is all connected, beloved child. Nothing is random. It is random for you, when you haven't yet seen the pattern. We are in the times of unravelling. It will all be revealed. The truth will set humanity free. No one can stop this from happening. It is eternal here where I AM. All patterns that trap you from not being, are clear to see and unravel. One day may you be free, as I AM. I love you.

It is all here and now.. There is no need to figure this one or anything out. There is no need to understand. All the information is already here and now. All you need to learn and master is how to breathe and how to listen deeply. As we have both been desiring from the beginning of time. I yearn to be in communion with you, my child. May you learn to listen to the silent whisper that I AM. We are in this together.. Every thought, every word and every agreement counts. Exponentially into the future of mankind. Thank you for being such a devoted archetype into the unravelling of truth. From the beginning of time, it is the word that creates worlds. *Your* words, every single one of them, is what will create the worlds to come.

"May we deepen our bond in-love and our communication. I pledge to continue to learn to surrender deeper into the listening of the great mystery that I AM. I pledge loyalty and devotion to you, creator of all in *me*. I pledge to focus on the harmony of nature that is beating inside of the heart that I AM."

May the promise that I AM, be true for all of you. I trust in the highest truth that I AM. I trust in unconditional love that I AM expressing itself. I trust in the expression of compassion that is the galactic superpower, inside of humanity, that is bringing us all together.

"I trust in the prophecies that have been perceived from the eye witness that I AM.
I trust in miracles and new timelines.
I trust that humanity will bring forth the blessings that we have all been waiting for.
The truth will set me free."

It is very simple but it is not that easy. We must first acknowledge the truth. We then need to accept the truth. To then embrace the truth and learn to love the truth as a part of us. Regardless of how barbaric and perverse the truth of the past can be. It is a part of you. The highest truth is also a part of you. Christ, the embodiment of God on earth, lives in you. You are the creator. Blessing the earth with *your* steps, *your* words and perception. May the Christ in you expand to walk, speak and see as I AM. 'Thank you dearly,' I say.

In the eternal perception of our creator. We are one and the same. Darkness and light are one and the same. It is only this moment. This particular snapshot of time, that we can witness. We are all inside of a unique contrasting experience. In truth, we are all in this together. *Your* unique experience today, will be someone else's tomorrow. This is why judgement and punishment is so far from the truth.

In the depths of *your* discovery. You have been navigating the darkest oceans where we face murder. All the sharp reactions around strong passions that can cut open the fibre of creation. You have experienced the whole human experience in this life, facing and feeling death through the experience of dying, being killed and killing. Witnessing sharp passions arising from deep inside. You know that it is coming from previous embodiments and this feels true. Then again you know that all of this exists within you. You recognise that punishing the murderer or the abuser is not wanting to see that this expression is also a part of you.

You recognise that it is only guilt and shame that punishes this person's actions. You recognise that healing from these dark passions is possible. It is possible when we accept and embrace the unity of all things. This is an important initiation to go through. It is not until we are at peace with death that we can truly be in the world of the living. It is from the land of the living that we can give the person, perpetrating, the opportunity of redemption and salvation. It is inside of judgement that you have been killing each other down.

$$\Omega$$

The unveiling of time is happening. Then again time is a very *tricky* energy to build a relationship with. In the end of times it is all different. I recommend you to discern and distinguish the limiting forces that anyone in form needs to work through. It is a *tricky* energy as the trickster of the mind has given us perceptions that are not true. Time is not linear and time doesn't end. Time exists in the cycle of day and night. Time exists in the cycle of growth. Time exists in the cycles of manifestation. Time exists whenever there is a process of gestation and manifestation.

Then again, in every moment, of everytime, everything that exists is right there where there is no time. The moment time disappears is the moment that anything can happen again. We get lost back in time. As we fear *something or nothing*. We leave the moment. We gain comfort in trusting the process of gestation and manifestation that we know.

It is an honour to witness this beautiful dance of being in eternity and coming back to where time exists. I am sure that many of you already know that time is not linear. In fact, in these times, the form of the spiral is quite accepted as the form of time. We go back to the past, and relive when we missed something.

Inside the path of realisation. There is not a conversation that will allow you to be free from time. Inside the collective unravelling. We are in-time. As whenever there is distance in space, there is time. Time exists, because separation exists. It is in *your* own sacred space, when the edges of form start to dissolve. Alone, is when we can access the space of *no-time*.

It takes for the inner child to get *it*. It takes for the inner child to have that *aha* moment. That moment when the *coin drops* and there is no time. You actually do not know when this will occur. Exactly as you don't know when the mental *aha* moments that you are already used to, will happen. Two very distinct and different conversations. For the inner child to have the "Aha moment." The whole body needs to be in agreement first. The mind speaks about the journey through our relationship with time. The body articulates, in the senses, the destination for transformation. The *aha moment* of transformation occurs when it does. We get it, as a full embodiment, when we get it.

🎵 Time keeps us sleeping, sleeping, into the future.
Time keeps us sleeping, sleeping into the future.
What you are going to do, with your time, it us up to you 🎵

Ω

In solitude and in a sacred space, I have found that this mantra, in meditation, is very powerful to open up blockages in the body that are limited by time. I have found that it is a swift way for the body to open to the eternal bliss that I AM now. - May you enjoy it:

Breathe

Breathe in: "I AM time."   Breathe out: ...silence...

Breathe in: "I AM time."   Breathe out: ...silence...

Breathe in: "I AM time."   Breathe out: ...silence...

Breathe in / Breathe out: "I AM time."

Breathe in / Breathe out: "There is no Time."

Breathe in / Breathe out: "I AM time."

Breathe in / Breathe out: "There is no Time."

Breathe in / Breathe out: "I AM time."

Breathe in / Breathe out: "There is no Time."

Breathe in / Breathe out: ...silence...

Breathe in / Breathe out: ...silence...

Breathe in / Breathe out: ...silence...

CO-CREATING THE NEW EARTH AS I AM

"I AM that I AM and as I AM. I share and extend all *my* blessings as far as this eye can see. As far as this heart can feel. I AM free. I AM sovereign. I AM love in movement and vibration. I AM a student of each moment. I AM abundant in health, love and livelihood."

In time. As the journey goes. The feminine essence of nature is preserved inside of you and the masculine essence of presence is built outside. They are in unison vibrating as one. Now embodying the vibrations of *your* desires. Accepting them. Honouring them and breathing them into existence. Inside no attachment of how the outcome should be. You have introduced the lower desires inside. To the higher desires. You have danced through the dissonance of separation. Dancing in *your* solar plexus, and meeting intimately with each other. Creating resonance. Dancing together in harmony.

Stay in this communion, dear child. Allow for the rewriting of the system to exist in you. As I AM. Breathe with me. This is the key to soothing and calibrating the body, back to its natural state. Breathe with me.

"I can't express enough gratitude to be able to write all these words so far. The last nine months have been the most truthful of times. If only one thing remains. I hope that you are left with this. Life happens through us. It is when I shape. In free-will. The sacred name of "I AM." That manifestation happens for us. It is in the spell of "I AM." That we can weave our vibrations towards our redemption and salvation. We can also weave towards the opposite spectrum in creation. The saturated space where invalidation of self prevails.

You are deep in the journey or you have started. Regardless. We are in this together. We are in *the cycles,* guiding each other back home."

As nonsensical as it can sound. Self-doubt is what has taken us this far. It has been pushing us to prove ourselves by making *things* happen where we can find ourselves. Answering our deepest questions. Self-doubt is an inquiry. Although it stems from invalidation and depreciation. It is also an innocent part of us guiding us out from the prisons the *self* has created to keep us *safe*.

This is why this book exists.This is why you are reading this far. Wherever you are, how can doubt exist? It actually doesn't. It literally can't. Yet here we are. Inside the *doubts* and the *maybes*. We pretend that we don't know of our existence, when in fact we are only buying, wasting or stealing time. We already know who we are. We are just making sure. Moment to moment. This is valid and a beautiful journey of self discovery. Regardless, doubt seems to continue to ignite the fire of our identities. Attempting to prove ourselves. We create drama and we share our gifts. We are yearning to receive the attention that we are desperately needing to heal. The child is yearning to be seen. You have been trapped. Not recognising the self-doubt below. Not having the power of communicating vulnerably. Now a tool for our liberation that we are just getting used to.

The certain and calm breath that I AM, brings us back home to the centre of creation. It is in this *recognition of self* that we bring peace and harmony back to our environments. The transformation happens very quickly.

"To be in the world and not from the world."

I am starting to recognise what dear Jeshua meant when he said 'to be in the world and not from the world.' I am present to the immense transformation that has occurred for *me* in writing this book. I see how a part of me wants to say *me*, 'what about *me*?' In this same space. I communes, and whispers; *I AM*.

Deep breaths of presence are now available with ease and grace. The connection of all in one. It is breathing subtly in the tip of *my* nose. This book has given me *my* natural breath back. I bring back all the gifts from this experience to *attach* back into creation.

Manifesting its intentions. I bring back the intention to move forward as an upgraded version of *my-self*. Integrated as a servant to the presence that I AM.

"Secure Attachment."

"The sacred heart speaks loudly in me. It calls for secure environments. Through crystal clear agreements. May the sacred heart and the sacred womb find the divine middle way. May we learn to honour each other. May we have the ability to have freedom in the unknown and security from the commitments that meet our souls' desires.

We are breaking free from spells and all the doctrine that tells us that *attachments* are *bad*. There is fundamentally nothing good or bad. There is the conscious realm and the unconscious realm. This itself makes the difference. May we all make conscious choices, every moment of every day."

What are you consciously attaching to? Dear beloved child?

I am attached to *my breath*. Breath is *mine*. It is the ultimate gift that my creator has given me.

I am attached to *my* creator. Our creator is the eternal

reflection that guides me through the seas of love.

I am attached to *this body*. I literally can't separate from this body. Unless I terminate the ultimate gift of breathing. This body is the eternal gift to transcend time and dimensions.

I am attached to *greatness*. I desire with all this body to expand and promote the greatness and glory of our creator that I AM.

I am attached to the *seed of creation*. I pursue through practice and sacred containers to heal the sacred seed of creation within me.

I am attached to *the greatest good*. However the greatest good looks like. I do not know the way. I follow the way. The way knows the way.

I am attached to *vision*. I am eternally grateful to be able to see the unseen. I desire to serve all the visions that navigate through me. May I discern, with wisdom, what are the roles that I am meant to show up for.

I am attached to *my* presence. It is the most selfless gift. Allowing me to be *myself* in freedom. Allowing me to choose who the *ultimate one* is serving: *Who am I serving?*

I am attached to *myself*. It gives me a solid container for everything else to happen from.

I am attached to *love*. It is who I am. It is the ultimate access to all that I AM. I say farewell to *the* dear beloved, who leaves in me.

I am attached to *this centre*. It is the eternal gift of space where nothing and everything is available to *me*.

I am attached to *nothing*. I rest in the peace of knowing nothing, and that I could have made all of this up. For the greatest good and the greatest good only.

I am attached to *nothing*. I liberate the breath of spirit within.

I breathe.

I let go of these attachments and know that I can *attach* to them again, when in *need* or in *doubt*.

I know that if I hold onto them, I lose the guidance and safety that they bring.

I recognise that all of this journey is wasted, unless I practise meditation daily.

I recognise that *I* and *We* are one and the same. It takes *heart attitude* to be in the fine-line of unity

I learn to breathe comfortably in the uncomfortable space of this divide.

I breathe.

This is the frontier of the current agreement of what it means to be a human being. This is leading the way, in presence, to new conversations. The greatest reflection that I choose daily is the reflection of I AM. As *my creator is*. I love as *my creator loves*. I breathe as *my creator breathes*. Every moment, I have the freedom to choose who I AM, and what will be manifested. I pray for the easeful expansion of this centre. Inside of this reciprocated, conscious and clear attachments. I am ready to finish this book and share *myself* with anyone that is in front of me.

"May we all learn the true freedom of love. As I am you, and we are all one."

Thank you for reading *me* as the human that I am.

As I merge into one. I am writing through a current positional discussion with a powerful man that is wounded and working through the body, as I AM.

Witnessing how this discussion takes me out of the centre, and the communion with you, *my creator*. I am witnessing how the dynamics of these discussions are fuelling the masculine *ego* illusion of righteousness and positional competition. I am observing a tyredsome side of me, impatiently dealing with the *masculine ego* that continuously operates *on top* of the wounded child.

Not yet knowing how to express ourselves powerfully *through the wounds*.

I hope that I can lead with this example. I am feeling a deeper desire to surrender to the healing of these fibres and coming back to love. I am clear that what *our creator* wants is a heartfelt and peaceful communion between us. Our creator wants to bring unity back into all these ancestral dynamics of division with position, perception, and righteousness.

I am clear that this particular connection envelops healing for the masculine in many. The sensations are ancient, sharp and primal. Entangled in old philosophy. Belief systems and cultural practices of invalidation. It is clear how unworkable all these human dynamics are. It is clear to see how it opens the body up to the lower realities; where fear, anger and comparison exist. It is clear that we are meant to connect in humility and guide each other back home to love. As we dance. Inside. Free from the historical wounding. I AM.

I take a deep breath and deeply release. I create a new agreement of love, for myself. In this connection. This opens up a pathway to be able to communicate and bring back the communion where communities thrive.

It is so true the work you are doing, my child. *Your* resilient pursuit of the embodiment of one. This is what makes communion and the great frequencies of heaven to be available on earth. Embodiment creates the law of attraction. As when there is no attachment to a form or outcome. The message is clear for me to create freely through you. *Your* body emanates crystal vibrations of *your* greater vision, Bringing forward manifestation. Inside of a free communion with others.

    Your vision for building community. *Your* vision for sacred sacral union. Y*our* vision to serve others back to unity and truth. *Your* vision to serve the creator that I AM. All of these visions are aligned and crystal in *your* heart centre. None of these visions are contradictory. They glorify the greatness that I AM. They take care of you, and bring you closer to me. Thank you, dear beloved. It is only a matter of *time* for all these vibrations to be visible. To start manifesting the dreams that you desire. In *your* life now, dreams happen. As you are able to hold these vibrations. Expanding from the centre. Feel the resonance of *your* heart carrying and guiding you forward. It is in compassion that you allow *yourself* to completely release these visions back into creation. Forgive the limitations, in *yourself* and others. All that is holding *your* true vibrations back. It is compassion that allows you to surrender the mind of judgement. Allowing you to perceive that we are all doing our best. It is with compassion that we can access the deepest spaces in the body of love.

    "Compassion is loving simply because of its existence."

"In the tree of this life. I have chosen not to be a branch, a leaf, or a flower. I have chosen not to be the trunk or the roots. I have chosen to be all the tree itself. Including the soil, the wind, the sun and the water that nurtures it. I have chosen the freedom to be and to be this freedom. As you choose, for me, in the moment, Holy Spirit.

My feet are touching the ground. I AM connected to the centre, below and above. I AM guided by the truth that I AM. Now present in the breath that I AM, I breathe. I see the enormous gifts that creation has for me in this state of being. The tests and tribulations will continue, as they do. It is *my* choice. For *my* greater good. To love and stay in the centre. To react and get back into the story that is looking to find itself. Regardless of *my* choices. It is all perfect, and our destiny will be fulfilled.

Being alone now feels so good and nurturing. The deep chaos in our emotions is now making sense. The pattern is clear. Now you are perceiving that this chapter, in *your* life of *alonement*, is coming to an end. It is time to create community again. It is for you to remain at ease, being open and receptive. Who is meant to be with you, will come to you. As a holy child, it is time to connect the tree that you are, deeply into the earth. It is time to manifest a global forest of men and women. Like you, children that are whole, free and holy. It is time to multiply blessings. All the blessings are available here and now, dear children.

The passion of building heaven on earth, or the new earth as some people describe the horizon of light, is manifesting its fruits. Around the world. This book for transformation is almost finished, and anyone that has read this far, has done considerable internal *shadow* work to reach this point, and be in the centre.

You are not alone, and there are tools and allies available for you to continue this path of transformation. Please continue reading until the end. You are one, in the many, making an impactful difference on the ground. The dream to come together as one holy tribe has never been stronger. Guiding each other back home. Back to love. All of you, together, are creating the resonance and heart connectivity that has been missing. Thank you, holy children!

As this book is writing me, rather than I am writing it.

It has become clear that I am now *a writer!* An *esoteric writer* some would say.

I have recently decided, in the centre that I AM, to start a transition out of care work, and to clearly speak into what reflects the passion and desire that naturally emanates from the centre of this being: To empower people, to break down walls, and to build self sustainable communities.

I have recently started to draft *my crystal offerings*. Inside the seas of love that we are all swimming through. Everyday. Many of us could be drowning. The truth will set me free. Always. The truth inside our sacred hearts, and sacred wombs. We need to be crystal clear, with each other. We do not always know how to show our truth. We are in this together.

"May your divine offerings to this world become crystal clear."

I am now writing inside a deeper and raw intimate space. Bringing light into the darkest spaces of self. For more of us to be sustainably back into our unique centre of truth, love and vision. It is time for the many to meet and harmonise our darkest corners.

In the physical realm. I am assisting people to navigate psychologically and somatically through their own maze of ideas, emotions and identity. Back to the clear and empowered truth, as I AM.

I am supporting groups to build *off-grid communities* from scratch. From finding the ideal property, structuring and organising the community requirements. To building the core agreements and foundations that will sustain the *test of time* for the community.

These offerings are naturally and symbiotically aligned with the true essence of the love that I AM.

"May all these blessings multiply."

I am speaking exclusively to you now, dear beloved. The one reading this far. Please, if you desire, write down what you see with these questions. Please be insightfully straight with *yourself*. There is nothing wrong with you. Please write down what is true for you. It is meant to support you through this maze of words. This is an exercise to align *your* vision, *your* actions and purpose. When you write all of this down. You will be able to see the information in *your* system, which is contradictory. Cancelling each other out. Be insightfully straight.

What is not working for you in *your* life?

What is working for you in *your* life?

What do you truly desire to be doing in *your* life that you are not doing?

What is truly important to you?

What are the qualities of the people that you want to share *your* life with?

What are the qualities of what you want to give to others?

What does your life, actually, look like? Describe your day.

Be present to the truth underneath, in between and over *your* answers. What words in this paper are cancelling out, what you value to be important? Sometimes it is easier to be clear with ourselves when we share our intimate truth with another human being. Make a choice if you need to do this exercise with someone else and even if you need to do this exercise at all. Trust *your* intuition.

The voice that speaks words when we are taking care of our body, our mind and our spirit becomes crystal. The qualities or the crystalline light happens, and continues to guide our way consistently, when we are in health.

    The highest vibrations appear for us, as we take care of our body with clean water and nutritious food. As when we take care of our body with stretching and fitness. As when we take care of our body with sunlight and touch. The highest thoughts appear for us, as we take care of our mind with meditation. As we take care of our mind with innocence and curiosity. As when we take care of our mind with a mantra for focus and discipline. The highest presence appears for us as we take care of our spirit with joy. As we take care of our spirit with truth. As we take care of our spirit by speaking our deepest truth in compassion. As we take care of our spirit with natural connection to the world.

As we take care of ourselves, as a whole, and not its parts, with gentleness and presence. We are treating ourselves to the God in you. You are acknowledging the infinite qualities that reside in you and choosing the qualities that you want to harness for that day. This is how you can daily cultivate the qualities that you desire to manifest in *your* life. As you continue to unravel the deep desire of being, as a holy human, creator of things. Speaking in clarity, thinking in freedom and feeling true love.

Indeed, my child. You are still yearning to be in full continuous health. Anxious and depreciation timelines have been historically taking you out of centre. This time it feels very different. This book has developed a much stronger sense of who you are. In truth, Providing you with a lot more space to create from. A deep sense of presence and peace is very present in *your* heart, and breath. From this transformational work.

I invite you to continue with *your* life, day by day. Enjoy and embrace the happening that is present in front of you. It is my own responsibility to create for you the life that wants to manifest through you. *Your* sole duties are to *your* health. To love in relationships, and, when invited. To show up, as you are. It is when I make the unfolding happen, right in front of you, when you will know that it is *your* time to commit to this manifestation. Inside the flow of creation.

During these moments. You are not yet responsible for anyone else's well being. Except *your* own, and who chooses freely to walk with you. What is best for you, is what is best for everyone else. As we have discovered together. It is in this simple duty of being that you help me to create the growth and evolution of life on earth.

You are now waiting patiently, dear child. You are waiting for the metaphorical, internal arrow. To be strong and aimed at God, our creator, inside of you.

This arrow has gone through its own trials and tribulations. It is now aiming straight and ready to be shot into God's heart within. The arrow in you is now clear to see the truth of who you are eternally now. As the truth of others as an extension of you. The arrow you have built knows that it needs to remain vigilant to the tricks coming through the mind, and the corruption of the seed. At ease, trusting the grace of our creator. Now, if you choose, it is a good time for you to walk together in the tribe that you love so deeply, or keep walking alone into the unknown. The misunderstandings have now cleared enough. We can walk back with grace into the crystalline field of unity that you have been creating together.

Regardless, *your* destiny will be fulfilled. You will be held by the divine field of unity that emanates from Christ within you. As you now know, in a tribe, the arrow in you will strengthen. The tribe will protect, challenge, empower and nurture you in the human experience that continues. You are happy with the bonds that you have in *your* life. It feels like a full circle, coming back to the people that you love the most. Yet a part of you does not feel met.

Regardless, keep listening, dear child. You are back home and ready to deal with all the misunderstandings that are making prisoners of so many humans. Inside the illusion of separation and the need to heal from our own past. You are ready to love the beloved people in *your* life without the forms of attachments. You are ready to love them, regardless, whether they are the ones that you're building a life with, or not.

Now, that you are back home, my child, with the beloved humans in *your* life. Feeling completely held by *yourself*, and ready to rebuild dreams. Before we finish this transmission of light. We are going to speak about the matters of *your* world.

May the many see the truth that I AM and the

truth of what I AM not. The times that we are in, collectively, are critical to the destiny of mankind in this new era. As the *awakened* ones to the truth within, you are key to guide the way through this matter that we are making sense of. Not as *woke* but as *awakened* beings. Not in the past tense but in the now, wake up my children!

The matter that we are in. It is in perfect divine order. Yet it is a mess right now, and it is this way because we are not seeing our own demons within. We haven't shed light into our own darkest corners. We haven't unmasked the *dark one* with its name, to see the truth within. The unnamed demons are unleashed to harm our relationships and hurt what we love the most. The *breathless one* has been very busy, convincing you that all these *demons* inside and out, are not real. They don't need to be named. Instead, you should take pharmaceutical drugs to stay numbed and *balanced*. You should always have an *open mind* to accept all the labels, to be *woke* and to belong to the *truth* outside. The agenda of the few being subliminal and, nowadays, quite explicitly pushed by the media and entertainment industries, into *your* belief systems.

I do not want you with an open mind, dear beloved. I want you with a focused mind. Manifesting *your* own true desires. I do not want you distracted, finding the language that will allow you to *belong* in the world of labels and illusions. This now is a visible agenda and it only fuels division in *your* heart. I want you to have an open heart instead. An open heart so you can dissolve all these labels of division back into the truth of love. Into the core truth that we are one.

The so-called *Woke Culture* of acceptance and inclusion through all the labels of division imposed on us, makes logical sense. However, it is subtly keeping *your* attention outside, and out of the holy centre where I AM. It is creating new labels so everyone feels included, however, this is only at the surface level. In truth it is further dividing you, where it matters.

Inside, your heart is getting divided. Inside is the reactive battles of racial, cultural and gender identities. New labels give *new minorities a* sense of inclusion. In fact you are all my children. You are all brothers and sisters. There are no *minorities* in the truth that I AM.

This reactive force has been very occupied confusing us, dividing us and controlling us with a very clever use of language. This has been happening for a long time now. In *human time* anyways. These forces have been systematically penetrating organisations. Manipulating the truth, in very subtle ways, so that the logical mind won't be able to pick up on the difference. It is over time that these subtle manipulations make a big wedge between the real and the unreal. Tempting, penetrating and possessing the hearts and minds of the many who are seeking for identity, power, or a sense of purpose outside of the centre where I AM.

Often this agenda is covert, leaving the many unbalanced and incomplete. *Thinking* that this support is sincere and without conditions. In these unbalanced times. You are the one being used by the *dark one* and all of its tricks are happening through you. Many times you don't even notice that it is happening. How free are you from the ordeals of the mind? How free are you from the battle within? How much love and nurture is in *your* heart? How grounded are you inside of *your* own infinite power? How much peace emanates through you?

Many of you, my children, are trapped in *your* minds. Perceiving from this existential uncertainty that has resulted in the many of you, having left the back door unattended. The back door is how spirit incarnates through you. As this door is unattended, the contractions and shadows of fear are invited to take over. Expressed as tightness, insensitivity and heaviness to *your* back. Thus not allowing for *your* wings to agape, and not allowing for your sacred heart to rest wide open.

As we guard our back doors and we see *the demons* in the eyes, name them, and love these fears for what they are. The brighter the light of our heart becomes. This back door has always been open. This is how we can embody our highest truths. Are we willing to have a look? Are we willing to name and love the unlovable. Not looking at our darkest fears and unlighted longings is not a good idea. It is only allowing for the very small, yet highly influential groups, to continue hijacking *your* centre that I AM.

The agenda of *Satan,* the *dark one* who lives

inside of you. Is to take your breath away and trap you in *your* mind. This way penetrating many aspects of the *human reality*. Many *trusted* human institutions, and many *trusted* public and private figures, knowingly or unknowingly are part of this agenda. Political, religious, economic, and sporting institutions have lost the purity of its foundations to human weaknesses. It has been, relatively, very easy for these forces to guide the many to a false existential reality. It is with millimetric language adjustments, inside of the core message that allows for shadows to take over. In time. This agenda of division has been pushed by *powerful* media outlets. Making the division, amongst you, to sound much bigger than what it actually is.

Trust me, children. There are a lot more of you doing the work for truth, on the ground, than the few ones, *worshipping Satan as God*. Pushing the agenda of division and confusion. There are many more of you expanding *your* hearts and taking on the revolution of love. I will give you, my children, some examples of the dark forces at play. I hope it can be clear for you what is happening and how this happened…

Throughout time, these forces have created ways to divide the perception of humanity, using ideology to divide us. Ideology in politics, economics, gender, race, religion and culture. Ideology that confines the main aspects of what makes a human being into a set of ideas that we should conform to. Political ideologies that have conveniently divided us into *Right vs Left. Conservative vs liberal. The individual vs the community*. Making us pick a side. Please wake up, children! These are only ideas. They are not actual *truths of being*. These are ideas that are distracting you from what is actually happening. Inside of you. As you are forced to pick a side. You lose the centre where I AM. As you are out of centre, the deception of these forces have an open door into the fertile soils of *your* soul.

Have no fear, beloved child. You have awakened to see a way through it. Strengthen the space in the centre of existence. Strengthen the heart centre where all the realms meet at once. Breathe into your back. Speak vulnerable truth. Surrender to the unknown. This is how we cultivate truth in our lives. In the centre where presence, breathe and equilibrium exists.

Throughout history. Some of *your* dear brothers and sisters have been trying to control you. As you have been trying to control others. Attempting to create agreements that divide so you can feel safe. Based on the perceptions of differences in gender, race, money and other layers of identity. It is a complete waste of time and energy, my children. How can it make sense to pursue truth and liberation, making labels fit into *your* own individual truth. This only divides you and hurts you from the inside. You fall into this machinery of propaganda from the fear of not belonging. If you are only a label inside of the whole; How can you be free to embrace it all? How can the mind trick you to think that you are free, whilst fighting against, or for, these ever multiplying labels of separation? You are all of it, as I AM. Can't you see!

Nothing is the way it seems. Except the judgements from ourselves. It is all continuously changing. We are inside a constant ebb and flow. From the high peaks to the low froths of creation. What we need, and what our community and country needs, is presence!

Presence to the ever changing phenomena around and inside of us, constantly arising. Out of centre, we get *triggered* and all of this language of division becomes valid. We are not present to see the phenomena so we fall into the bait. Out of our centre, we are only creating more of the world of confusion and disconnection. This is the creation that comes from this machinery of separation. No matter how wise we sound. We need to know the matter to transcend the matter.

However, in the matter we can only stay in the conversation of matter. Time to let the matter go, dear beloved. Time to let go of that conversation. It doesn't matter. May you be free. May you learn to forgive with all of the heart. Knowing is not how we get out. It is in Love how you free back into the spirit that I AM.

"Are you now crystal of who I AM, dear beloved?"

This answer also doesn't matter, only this moment does.

A deep breath of release is felt throughout

As we are getting ready to finish this book. Something else happened today, dear beloved. Something that you have been waiting to feel and integrate for some time. This is what I witnessed: You are in a sacred space, and you choose to surrender to *your* touch. From practice, *your* touch has now mastered a gentle presence that touches pure love and heals the body. You have mastered a sense of touch to feel and listen to the deepest fibres of *your* being. You embrace the feminine within. The woman in you feels completely held and surrendered. She feels seen and felt. She surrenders like never before. You surrender and you hold in one, a gentle and sweet embrace. This creates a very deep phenomena of transformation, and you are suddenly taken over by the feminine force in you. It wants to fully express and liberate itself. You allow the happening to happen. Spirit starts to sing through you. Beautiful, deep and primal sounds start to find harmony through *your* voice. The force of nature appears in all its might. It starts to flow through you. It happens all at once. This cracks open the centre to *your* deepest truth in this body. You have been doing a lot of internal work for this phenomenon to happen.

It is happening now. You are in the most vulnerable of spaces. You feel safe. The eye in you scans the body with a gentle gaze and breath. The body is buzzing with light. The body is melting with love. The wounding, stored in the body, appears to be seen because it wants to heal. You witness the existing disconnection with *your* right leg. The wound of child abuse appears in the field. You remember all that you have worked through, in a moment. Rage arises and fills the body with heat. You stay with it. It quickly vanishes. Spirit asks for patience and takes over to show you something new. A new layer opens up, showing you the truth of this disconnection. A deep known fear of being sexually attracted to boys appears. It is what you have been hiding there all along. Only making the disconnection gap with the masculine, in you, wider. You know this. You have been here before many times. You have found shame, and a swift way to hide this truth again ... and again ... and again.

This time you are in the centre. This time it feels very small and innocent. This time, you've got this. You are calm and at peace, in the centre. You are ready to receive this truth and go deeper to the truth that I AM. What did you witness, my child?

"Wow. As I gently touched and communicated with the body. I saw. Below the story and wound of being a victim. How the small bones that stick out from my hips, have small pressure points that hurt a lot. I saw that it is here where the stories of desire for women reside on my left, and shame from a possible desire for men resides on the right. I allowed this feeling to play out and allowed myself to feel attraction towards the masculine. This feeling played out, allowing me to go deeper. This allowed for the attraction for men and women to balance out in the centre. In the centre I feel an enormous attraction to myself and to this moment. I release these attractions to go deeper. I find the eternity of peace, inside a connection with the root centre. I haven't felt this before. I had only found this profound peace with a connection to the heavens.

A new open space appears. I create a new agreement with our mother earth. A deeper commitment toward each other. I create a deeper surrender. Furthering *my* connection with the heavens in me. This activated centre feels at ease and grounded. I embrace this experience with a deep breath of gratitude. In the deep silence, I feel whole and I feel light."

Then what happened, my child? This is *yours* to share.

"Ok so inside this space of bliss, the holy spirit says, 'Not so fast. Remember the rage?'"

I then scan the body. The eye and heart discern what is in that moment. I feel ready and blessed to transmute this rage and find its truth. I am ready to free up this aggressive charge that hurts me.

This time around, it is brighter and the *thing* that calls itself rage. It also feels smaller than ever before. I witnessed a sensitive boy inside. A sensitive boy desperately finding anger as the only tool to get people to respect the boundaries that I needed to be respected. I witnessed a boy feeling protected from the outer disruptions. It is through people feeling unsafe that they then started to ask for *your* consent to come close.

I witness the mind maturing and a personality of firm boundaries developing on top of that anger.
I witness how this personality is what has pushed love away and ultimately hurt the people that I love. Particularly hurting myself.

"It felt very real and detached to witness this story. It felt easy to release this in the deepest of breaths. It felt particularly easy ro remind myself 'I AM eternally safe.'"

You breathe and integrate safety into the body for some time. You are now back to a regulated centre. You witness *yourself* being more surrendered in the heart. The heart space feels safer and wider. Thank you, dear beloved child.

"The breath in me feels now in a wider and in deeper ease. Grace is present. Inside this bliss, spirit shows that this is a tender space to be explored lightly.

The strongest of fires is and will continue to be present in me."

You feel the familiar human space again and you come back to embodying what is now present for you. There is so much more space than before. Thank you, dear beloved. The human experience continues. *Your* vibrations are attracting new life. We meet in the centre, wherever you are now. We meet and meet again.

Now, my child, let us complete this task. Let's get real back and into the body. You are *tired. Your* internal work to find the true flow of God that you are, is complete.

The shadows inside of you feel safe. Many shadows in you, are ready to be with me, in the light, and are receding out. It is time to rest and get our hands dirty with our mother. It is time to embody the wholeness of all that you are. You are now breathing in unison between the seed below and the heart above. You are clear that this is how it is meant to feel. The embodiment of the divine masculine. The seed feels at home connecting with the heart. The heart feels at home while you are breathing into this space peace,the light and balance of presence.

It is time now to show the light that you are to the world, dear child. You are in presence as it is. What does it look like? Share with us the flavour of *your* authentic practice moving forward. What do you want to share now and give completion to this process of mastery?

"I am writing the day before my 45th birthday. I am finding the true word within. Everyday, I practise being in presence. Every day there are seeds of doubt and fear that want to grow in the mind. I daily plough them out of the soil of the earth that I am within. Each day there is a new space to create on this fresh earth. I consciously plant back into the empty spaces. I plant seeds of love, and I water them with love. In the form of *care and attention*.

I give myself the time to sit still, outside of any time. Until the mind is quiet and observing what is right in front of me. I let this go as it wants to go. Once I am without a thought. I stay still in this space until the breath in me is touching and soothing all of the heart space and I can register that I am.

Once the heart is full. I stay still until the bliss in this space connects with the sacred seed below. Once it connects and the kundalini is awakened. I tuck in the navel to give the sacred energy that I am back to myself.

I stay still with this breath bringing communion in between the heart and the seed. Once this communion is felt, I stay with this presence learning from the divine connection between the higher and the lower. In between heaven and earth. In between the heart and the seed of life. From this space I am deep in the centre. Feeling the raw sensations that this heart space wants to alchemise and release this day. I feel the deep love that I have for all the beloved, I release all these feelings with form, into a visual golden perspective of embodied light and expansive flight for *myself*.

I feel the love, and all the incomplete conversations that the heart space is requesting from me to deal with in communication. I discern when these conversations are needed, and when silence and alchemy will bring further blessings to that connection.

I am deep in the centre that I am. From this place I feel the presence of the almighty I AM. The sweet breath in the tip of this nose. The ever present presence of silence and unconditional love that I meet with this breath, I am meeting now inside this heart.

From this practice, the illuminated heart appears to grow in the breath and the presence of peace and balance. From this expanding light, the peaceful and balanced heart, carries these qualities to the lower and the higher realms of this body.

The peaceful and balanced body of light expands and connects with the unconditional love outside. Creating heavenly bonds on earth with other vibrations that resonate in that same frequency.
A pathway for this day becomes clear.

I start my day, walking and connecting with all the directions. I sit still, and focus on the tasks for the day. "What can I do today that is for the greatest good of myself and everyone?" I make the calls, write the emails and meet the people that I am crystal clear about.

Some days I only rest. I trust in being divinely guided and I continue to listen. I am building up the magnetism of this presence and holding space in this heart for the blessings to come."

Are you in doubt this far, dear beloved?

You also have an illuminated heart, dear child. It has never stopped shining. If there's doubt, it is only the mind masking the winds of desire and contractions from fear, shame and guilt that you have inherited, and have not yet seen.

It is perfect as you are, dear beloved. Keep practising the dissolution of the illusion. All of this new matter and all of these deeper emotions are now alleviating us from the seed that doubts existence.

You exist, there is no doubt. You are right here in the presence of all that you are, and all that you think that you are. Reading this exact word right now.

I surrender to this presence that I AM. I protect this vessel and this heart. I practise the presence of *I AM*.

I reconnect with a source of truth when in doubt.

I am grateful for all the heavenly protection that is with me. I am devoted to our sacred mother right here in me, and our sacred father in heaven, also inside.

My gratitude to them is by acknowledging this birthright and liberating the golden child within.

In the light, I am cheeky. I am funny and I love to play and create. I love to poke the trees so the fruits fall and become available. I love to build with friends. I love to serve the people that I care for. I love to be with God.

In the shadows, the natal *Pluto Complex* unravels a firm and scared lion that roars to the unseen chaos to be seen. Sometimes inside the fear of getting hurt or swept away from truth. Sometimes as a servant of Zion.

I am growing in love with the shadows and its dance finding its own light that is eternally everywhere. I carry the torch forward. Into the shadows. As the holy spirit asks from this I that I am. I have the natural courage, and sensitivity, to look deep into the chaos. Even when it seems frightening. I only feel safe because I am with the spirit that I AM that is everywhere at once.

I am learning to have deeper compassion for all that I AM. The holy spirit asks that I fulfil the destiny of this book. Asks me to go through this book again entirely, in presence, 3 times! The holy spirit asks me to fill the heart space with compassion from the transmisión of the light that I AM. I accept. I recognise how much resistance I am feeling to go through it again. I am *tired*. The holy spirit speaks loudly through the centre of the heart.

"Nothing to worry about. You have developed seeds of compassion throughout this book. You are only bringing more crystalline energy to *your* life, and the life of others, by going through this book again. The unravelling is not complete."

I recognise that compassion is what allows humanity to show the way forward. Uniting the rest of the galaxies within. I recognise that this body needs the sweet honey of compassion to soothe and regenerate its somatic fibres back into one.

We have put this body through the hard work to go through the eye of the needle and crack open the mustard seed that we have been searching for. It is done. May I continue the path of forgiveness, and *holy union,* through this centre in me…

It is time to bring further flexibility to where I AM rigid. It is time to water, with the love that I AM, the root cause of the rage that I am experiencing. I can see the origin of the rage in this body. I can see how it has been *protecting me.*"

"It is time now to rest and show up in the world as the world calls you."

The first time that you exploded with all of *your* fire towards the shadows of this world. You expressed it through the closest ones to *your* heart. It is time to water all that you are, with the sweetness of compassion

You can see how this rage is valid and protects the sacred. Yet it has been keeping you in the shadows, as a man. Blocking the heart from liberating. This rage is ancestral. Men and women have been relating in the shadows for way too long. Own, dear children, the despair that is holding you back! The pain that doesn't allow you to be full hearted. Feel it, in stillness, until it is gone. Sing and create vibrations. Let it out! Open up! Activate! I love you feeling *your* most intimate.

It is time for you to continue this journey and grow in trust. Men are hurt from being continuously corrected by their connection with their mother. Left, with an emotion in the core of the heart, as not being good enough. Women are hurt by men's lack of presence, not being able to feel secure and trust men and even God. In the centre, we can hold all the energy in motion that goes through, and purifies our environments.

"May this book bring light and liberation to the many."

"I am freeing myself from the web of judgement, and I recognise that any word that I write or speak does not help me to do so. Love is the way through. If there is a need to express love in language. This only shows that I am not yet fully embodying its vibration.

I am eternally a student, learning the way. I recognise that it is time to complete this story of eternal love that I AM. It is time for me to live simply and profoundly love all that is. One moment at a time. Inside no distinction but love itself. Inside the container that I AM.

I recognise the importance of letting go of this story and the destiny of this book to be as it is meant to be. I recognise that this story has just started and there is no separation between these words and what is alive inside of me. I recognise that I will continue to breathe the love that I AM. Felt as compassion, patience and truth. Into the doubts that arise everyday.

I recognise that being human is the greatest gift there is. I am a creator. Made in the image and likeness of my creator. I have the ability, through the unique gift of compassion. To create the unity field for creation. I recognise that love is a verb and a noun. It is in action and presence that we create worlds."

The end is here, dear one, and it is only the beginning.

"May we all join the revolution of love."

What is the invitation, my child?

"I invite the reader to share the golden insights that you got from this book. Make it real for you.
I invite everyone that has read this far. To go through the acknowledgments and recommendations section. We have published clear and direct invitations to access tools and initiatives that can further advance this intention for transformation on our planet."

"May this divine transformation for *myself*, and for the *many*, happen as it is written in heaven."

USE THIS SPACE

THE MANIFESTATION OF NUMBERS

Dissecting 'I AM that AM' inside the primal numbers of manifestation. For the *nerds,* like *me*, that love the entertainment of the pondering mind. I am exploring the power of words. The sequence of numbers, as the teachers from the past, have shown me. It feels good to give it all away.

"Holy Spirit, please protect this creation with *your* mantle of light. May all the heavenly realms guide its process of manifestation. May it serve as many people as possible. May all beings in all the worlds be happy."

At the beginning there was nothing ...

Void
                   0

Then came the word ...

"I."
                   1

The word created consciousness ...

"I AM."
                1-2

The conscious word then created a sense of resilience, inside of duty ...

"I AM a Clear Channel."
                1-2-3

The word then creates form ...

"I AM clear channel to write this book."
                1-2-3-4

The word then creates the witness in time, a purpose.

"I AM writing this book for the healing of this body."
1-2-3-4-5

The word then manifests balance outside, and inside of its purpose.

"I AM writing this book so it can serve as a blueprint for the healing of many."
1-2-3-4-5-6

The word then creates an opportunity.

"I AM writing this book and I AM sharing it worldwide."
1-2-3-4-5-6-7

The word surrenders to all that is possible for this creation

"I AM offering this book for the greatness and glory of creation and as its creator."
1-2-3-4-5-6-7-8

The word manifests the full spectrum of this possibility.

"I AM writing this book for it to be read, and for its light to spread, in every continent on earth."
1-2-3-4-5-6-7-8-9

The word speaks its presence

"The light that I AM in this book is spreading everywhere."
1-2-3-4-5-6-7-8-9-10

The word produces presence.

"I AM spreading the word of this book through many outlets for promotion."
1-2-3-4-5-6-7-8-9-10-11

The word manifests presence

"I AM witnessing the light of this book present in all continents in the world."
1-2-3-4-5-6-7-8-9-10-11-12

The word is the presence that I AM

"I AM made of spirit as this book is made of me. I AM you and you are me. There is nothing in between us."
1-2-3-4-5-6-7-8-9-10-11-12-13

It is done. It is done. It is done

ACKNOWLEDGEMENTS & RECOMMENDATIONS

In this section, I am acknowledging the many human beings that have aided and inspired me through this process of expansion; Into the truth of love. You know who you are, and you are an intrinsic part of this heart that I am.

After, trialling many disciplines and discerning what is real and what is not. I am also recommending what has worked for me that I truly want to promote. May you continue on *your* journey to come out from the shadows.

Disclaimer: Please note that these are only my personal recommendations, and do not constitute any sort or form of formal advice. I am not offering professional advice, these are only my views and opinions from my own experience. .

Acknowledgments:

I want to acknowledge the many wise men and women who I have met, and who have guided me through the years. Through the writing of this book. *Your* music, *your* words, *your* listening, your love! Thank you greatly for being part of this book. You know who you are. You have supported and will, probably, continue to support guiding me back home.

I want to acknowledge all the women of this life that have shown me who I am. Inside intimacy in the different stages of my development. Thank you so much for showing me and continuing to show me what true love is and how a true man looks like.

I want to acknowledge our elders past, present and emerging. As I acknowledge the original custodians of the lands that we are walking on. I want to personally acknowledge where I am. The Bundjalung Country. The original custodians of this land where I live. They have welcomed me into their country, inside the vast land of 'Australia' and its over 500 indigenous nations.

Personal recommendations:

- **LionMedicine Coaching:** if you feel an unquestionable pull to continue working with me. You can make contact and book a session.
  I offer transformational and sacred spaces in 1-1 virtual sessions. If you are interested to know more, please visit: www.lionmedicine.com

- **Community Funding - ONIS:** we are keeping this non-for-profit initiative alive. If there is interest, we will launch a social media network where we support each other to buy land and create community. We have started this before, and it is not worth starting, unless we are one million members. Please express *your* interest in this link below. We will launch the platform and send you an invitation to join, as we reach one million expressions of interest. www.onis.life

- **Community Building:** I am personally very passionate about promoting and supporting all who are looking to buy land and create intentional and sustainable off-grid communities. I also recommend these resources as a great place to start finding the tools that you need to create *your* community: www.ecovillage.org www.ecovillages.au

- **Men Initiations:**. This movement is global and this organisation operates with utmost integrity and responsibility to create a powerful and healing container for men. It is a profound difference to walk together with our fellow brothers: www.mankindproject.org

- **Mastery in Integrity and Word:** this organisation operates in the strictest integrity that I have encountered. The reason being is that they are holding space for others to gain access to the world of integrity. This organisation gave me the ability to have easeful access to my blindspots, and an easeful authority over the minds' chatter: www.landmarkworldwide.com

- **Plant Medicines:** Plant medicines as allies for healing are becoming more widely spread and accepted. A plant ally is as common as the drink that you have in the evenings. It is important to discern and choose what is best for you. You will attract the practitioners and servers of plant medicines, based on *your* own level of integrity. This is a very sensitive practice and brings risks to mental health if not done with complete duty of care. We hope to create or attract a crystal clear website, with resources for plant medicine integration and what to keep an eye out. God willing this will be available in future editions.

- **World BookTour:** if this experience touched you and sparked the light in you. We invite you to spread the word of this book for transformation. If it made a difference to you. You can support this message by sharing with *your* friends and family, by becoming a member of the "friends of the book club," and by promoting online through *your* social media. Please visit: Crystallighthouse.org

- **Christ lineage mystery schools:** the truth of the unconditional love that has been shaded by religion, with code, is appearing now in "crystal form." It is happening all over the world. In future editions, God willing, we will include these resources.

- **Crystal Lighthouse Publishing:** It is committed to using the profits of this book, and other books that Alejandro writes. To promote community centres around the world that foster the healing and liberation of self expression. Please visit us for more information. Crystallighthouse.org

-

NAMASTE

The divine in me bows to the divine in you

www.ingramcontent.com/pod-product-compliance
Lightning Source LLC
Chambersburg PA
CBHW060548080526
44585CB00013B/485